Black Love Matters

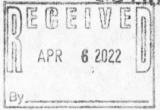

Black Love Matters

Real Talk on Romance, Being Seen, and Happily Ever Afters

EDITED BY JESSICA P. PRYDE

BERKLEY

New York

BERKLEY
An imprint of Penguin Random House LLC
penguinrandomhouse.com

PUBLISHER'S NOTE

For Deirdre and Delores.
For putting books in my hands
and love in my heart.

Contents

Introduction

When I was eight years old, I used to pretend that the kiss on the tarmac was the final scene of *The Bodyguard*. (Don't ask why I was watching an R-rated movie at eight; I had my ways.) The giant swell of Whitney Houston's powerhouse version of Dolly Parton's "I Will Always Love You" makes the perfect fade-out for my own ending to the 1992 movie, one where Kevin Costner's secret-agent-turned-bodyguard Frank Farmer doesn't move on to another job, recovering from the bullet he took. Where Whitney Houston's Oscar-winning triple threat Rachel Marron doesn't literally fly off into the sunset, future unknown. Long, rotating kiss shot, hit that high C, roll credits, end of story.

I might not have thought about it this way then, but I was giving Rachel—giving *myself*—a happy ending, one that I could be satisfied with as a burgeoning devourer of love stories. And the fact that it was a Black woman I was giving the happy ending to, in such opposition to the other media I'd been exposed to and would continue to experience for the next few years, was no small factor in *needing* to see that happy ending. (I can also rewrite the narrative in my mind as an adult to consider that while Frank doesn't work for Rachel anymore, they can still be together. Just not all the time. But that's another story.)

I've rewritten a few narratives in my head—and spent a lot of time reimagining those narratives that are, thankfully, on obsolete technology and can never be accessed ever again—but continue to work hard to seek out my own kind of representative love story. I've been lucky enough to come across those stories at a young age, first on-screen—from Purlie & Lutiebelle to Sparkle & Stix to Martin & Gina—and later on the page, mostly in books borrowed from and returned to the library as a tween that I'll never remember the titles of but always remember how they made me feel. Love stories centering the Black experience aren't the only thing I read, but when I find the great ones, the feeling is the absolute best.

But even with that feeling bursting in my veins, I can still acknowledge that for Black people, especially in the United States, a happily ever after hasn't always been easy to come by, and continues to present challenges.

For more than four hundred years, people of African descent have been treated abysmally in many nations of the world. We've been denied citizenship, jobs, housing, voting rights, equality, equity, respect, and often, common human decency from our fellow humans. Yet, whether free or enslaved, Black people throughout history have been able to find romantic love—regardless of their ability to marry—both inside and outside their own communities. They created their own kind of hand-fasting and married for themselves, if nowhere else but in the eyes of a god—or in their own eyes, if a higher power wasn't something they could believe in.

But because of institutional racism and a white supremacist society, Black consumers were often exposed only to white love. If there was a person of color from any background in a book or film centering a white narrative, they were often given a more tragic ending—death, the death of their lover, their death *at the hands of* their lover, killing their lover, being left behind by a lover, and killing their child. There were exceptions, often in media produced either by or with great input by creators of color. "Race pictures" and novels written by Black creators developed their own popularity within the Black community but weren't considered works of the canon until long after the deaths of the people involved in their production. Instead, Black consumers were expected to fall for the white narratives of love and romance that were offered to them. (This is, perhaps, why the Saturday afternoons of my youth, spent with my grandmother, often featured the likes of romantic films starring Clark Gable and Mario Lanza, on top of the more tragic tales—*West Side Story, A Warm December, Carmen Jones*—that littered her own film history.) In modern times, the Black consumer remains in search of stories about people like ourselves falling in love. Many of us are just as happy—though maybe not as satisfied—with stories about others doing so.

We have to be.

Because for too long, for too many of us, those stories have been the only option.

In 2018, I picked up a copy of Glory Edim's *Well-Read Black Girl*, which collects points of view from Black readers and authors from all walks of life reflecting upon seeing themselves in fiction. It was a meaningful, well-put-together collection. But what I noticed, as I read those essays and followed the ongoing list of WRBG Book Club selections, was a lack of romance. These women weren't (openly) romance readers, and romance wasn't included in the scope of "well-read" for these particular Black girls. The idea for the collection compiled here, which had been only a nugget in my ever-revolving wheel of potential ideas, sprang fully formed in an initial essay (okay, maybe it was a bit of a tirade) about the place of Black romance readers in the greater scope of Black readers and the world. I eventually came back to it with a cooler head, and I could see the path that lay before me: What had other romance readers in my position experienced? What did they have to tell the world? What other types of love story, other types of love, have made an impact on Black readers, Black viewers, Black consumers of popular culture from blockbuster films to Twitter? How does the need for a Happily Ever After affect us all, no matter our own background or current situation?

One thing was and continues to be clear: we could all use a little more joy. The generational trauma built into our DNA has lasting impact. No matter what our life journeys, we still share the lived experience of being Black in a world where there is still racial suffering, racial tension, and racial social disparity.

Whether we enjoy reading books about characters similar to ourselves—an enjoyment that many of us realize, like a flashing spark of light, the moment we first discover one—or embrace every world and universe provided to us by popular culture, we find something worth delighting in. Badass, feminist protagonists; competent humans who can live well-rounded, complex lives and still want love; hot messes who figure themselves out with the help—or despite the hindrance—of those around them. People who grew up how we grew up, who got the same speeches from their mothers, or had the same reasons to side-eye their bosses.

ROMANTIC LOVE HAS been one of the most essential elements of storytelling for centuries. Most people in the modern era have grown up on a steady diet of fairy tales and popular culture featuring the lasting power of true love and its kiss. Desire for that perfect kind of love, that happily ever after at the end of the story, is an almost universal trait for people from all walks of life. But for Black people in the United States and across the diaspora, depictions of love and romance—both true and fictional—have been hard-won for the entire five centuries that people of African descent have been in the New World. And for the same number of centuries (and probably for centuries to come), those who were part of the majority culture didn't see anything wrong with that, because they "couldn't identify" with characters who didn't look like them. In modern times, the Black consumer remains in search of stories about people like themselves falling in love.

According to the Pew Research Center, the person most likely to read a book in the United States is a college-educated Black woman. And to bastardize Jane Austen a bit, it is a truth prevalently acknowledged that a Black reader of any gender in possession of literary wokeness must be in want of novels by the great storytellers of Black life: Toni Morrison, Alice Walker, Zora Neale Hurston. Of memoirs centering social justice from Roxane Gay and Assata Shakur. These goddesses of Black womanhood present compelling, meaningful stories that make us deeply consider our own lives, and are important voices in our newfound modern canon. For ages to come, people will read their elegant, heavy-hitting analyses of the truths of Black life in America and around the world.

As much as we need these books, we—as readers, viewers, consumers—deserve joy in our lives alongside the hard truths many prominent Black voices posit. We already have such a traumatic history, filled with stories featuring the constant loss of love, or the idea that we don't deserve romantic happy endings (or any kind of happy ending at all). And so we turn to love stories. Love stories about women in control of their lives and sexuality, who are allowed to be desired and uplifted, and who get the happy ending they deserve. About Black men who don't have to succumb to the toxic masculinity that society enforces and enables. Stories about people of all backgrounds and identities who might suffer but who don't *have to suffer* for the sake of the plot. We all have stories, and not one of them is the same. But we share a passion for love stories that brings us together in many different ways.

Black love stories (especially with happy endings) have long had a fraught road to publication. Thanks to the segregation of television and film media that continues to persist, we have not had our share of positive examples of love . . . but there are still enough standout examples to name down the line. We can harken much further back to a common language of Black cinema than we can to that of Black romance novels, thanks to a parabolic ebb and flow of screen media. The classic films that were made for the broader American Cotton Club began the journey, but it wasn't until the 1990s that we began to see a large influx of fun, relatable stories about Black people from different walks of life finding each other and love. Nowadays, we are beginning to see a small renaissance of Black films and shows, which take the cultural clarity of that golden era to the next level of thought, cultural competency, and social justice. And much like everything else in this day and age, the love stories are just that much more intense, more angsty. But no less satisfying when that happy ending is reached. Even if it's a Happy For Now.

In print literature as a whole, we spent a long time finding the nuggets of happiness in the more "serious" literature expected of Black authors as publishing maintained its requirement of Black Exceptionalism. Many of the stories that revealed a happy, happening Black community of the past were lost to the greater world due to small print releases and the loss or near-loss of authors' archives. Even now, we are discovering works of authors long and recently dead that change the way we see Black life in the twentieth century and before. And in the romance genre, when the concept of happy Black people in love met the opposing ears of publishing gatekeepers, it was the work of editors like Vivian Stephens that allowed Black authors to have a place in category romance and genre romance publishing as a whole.

There are people who might not have been *readers*, let alone readers of romance, if not for romance novels featuring Black characters. Thanks to lifetimes of overexposure to the White Norm, there are plenty of people who have lived their lives under the preconceived notion that romance as a genre is Not For Them. For many, the books they see on the shelves of bookstores and libraries, on the web, in other people's hands, indicate they might not have much, if anything, in common with their protagonists—ironically, the same Othering argument that white supremacist readers have espoused about "Black books" for years. But in the case of the Black reader, finding just one book that *is* for them is life-altering. It opens doors to a fifty-year history of stories featuring Black people in love. And no version of this discovery is insular. This is the reader who will share what they have found, wanting trusted confidants to share in their newfound joy. The reader who, in their excitement, will share the source of their delight with the world. On any social media platform, you can find a post from a Black reader expressing surprise and delight at finding such a treasure . . . and wanting more.

But.

Over 90 percent of the books offered by traditional publishers in the romance genre are not about Black people in race or experience.

According to The Ripped Bodice's 2020 Report on the State of Racial Diversity in Romance Publishing, 8.1 percent of books published by established romance publishers and imprints in the previous five years were by authors of color—a category that includes non-Black authors, sending the number of Black authors down even further. Ripped Bodice owners Bea and Leah Koch's acquisition of information isn't perfect, but they're the only numbers we have that are specific to traditional romance publishing. They also do not encapsulate the massive growth of Black and interracial romance being published independently by Black authors through platforms like Amazon. Black authors who publish exclusively on their own or who alternate between traditional publishing and self-publishing don't get the same up-front pay guarantees that traditional publishing promises (to whatever extent they might receive advances and high royalties), but they have complete control over the stories they want to tell. So, on one hand, we can take that low number of traditionally published romances and shame the publishing industry for being so disproportionately white-focused. But on the other, we can acknowledge that this gatekeeping has allowed us access to stories that might be more true to any number of Black experiences.

Even with the ever-growing outlet of romance featuring Black protagonists, the life and experience of the Black consumer is inherently intersectional. It becomes even more so when sexual and gender identities are brought into play. Love stories are for everyone. Romance novels are not just by women, nor are they solely about straight couples. Black consumers who are beyond the allocishet "norm" must search harder, look deeper, to find their community. And just as before, we must take different avenues to find the mirrors *and* windows that will offer us a safe and enjoyable experience—free from not only the race-based trauma that literary fiction might present, but also free from overly heteronormative, homo- and transphobic narratives that are still commonplace in genre romance.

No Black consumer is the same, but every contributor to this essay collection has experienced a similar awakening to the importance of the HEA, whatever that looks like, for people of all kinds. For some, that has included pulling their own chair to the table. For others, it has been more about setting up their own table and inviting others to join. Whether they are members of the romance community or overall consumers of media, they have integral positions on the concept of Black love and how it is presented to the world. These essays will discuss those varied experiences, from the perspectives of romance consumers and the Black authors whose books they devour, from creators and creatives who have both seen and made the love stories we all share.

———————

AS MEMBERS OF a society that is growing increasingly educated, increasingly queer, increasingly invested in social justice for all people, the examples we see in our romantic fiction help us to realize that it's not all hopeless, and that we have work to do. And in the end, it comes down to this: there is something utterly transformative about being exposed to Black Love—whether in a book, on a screen, or in real life.

The world is changing; while we still don't have more than a few options in every category of romance novel, the number of Black authors and readers continues to grow. And with that number comes a growing understanding of the Black Love experience, and the experiences of those who love Black people. The Black romance reader or media viewer of the future will not be scorned or dismissed because they dare to question the overwhelming whiteness of a creator's world. Their experience will continue not to match that of their white counterparts, because that has never been the goal.

The goal, in the end, is to impress upon those who most need it that Black Love matters. That Black people have full, meaningful lives, and that, in a world that hasn't often allowed it to us, Happily Ever After is ours to grab hold of, to wear against our hearts.

It's the least we deserve.

Black Love Matters

A Short History of African American Romance

BEVERLY JENKINS

Slave narratives were the first instrument used by African Americans to tell their own stories, so, in order to examine the history of African American romance, we must begin there. One of the earliest narratives my research turned up was one by Briton Hammon, published in 1760. It's memorable for the title's content and its length:

> *A Narrative of the Uncommon Sufferings, and Surprizing Deliverance of Briton Hammon, a Negro Man,—Servant to General Winslow, of Marshfield, in New-England; Who Returned to Boston, after Having Been Absent Almost Thirteen Years. Containing an Account of the Many Hardships He Underwent from the Time He Left His Master's House, in the Year 1747, to the Time of His Return to Boston.—How He Was Cast Away in the Capes of Florida;—The Horrid Cruelty and Inhuman Barbarity*

of the Indians in Murdering the Whole Ship's Crew;—The Manner of His Being Carry'd by Them into Captivity. Also, an Account of His Being Confined Four Years and Seven Months in a Close Dungeon,—and the Remarkable Manner in Which He Met with His Good Old Master in London; Who Returned to New-England, a Passenger in the Same Ship.

Try putting that title on a book today.

Narratives by women don't show up until more than half a century later, in 1831, with Mary Prince, a West Indies–born woman whose dictated story became Great Britain's first published account of an enslaved Black woman's life:

The History of Mary Prince, a West Indian Slave. Related by Herself. With a Supplement by the Editor. To Which Is Added, the Narrative of Asa-Asa, a Captured African.

Her story was published as calls for the abolition of slavery were on the rise.

I was immediately sent to work in the salt water with the rest of the slaves. This work was perfectly new to me. I was given a half barrel and a shovel and had to stand up to my knees in the water, from four o'clock in the morning till nine, when we were given some Indian corn boiled in water, which we were obliged to swallow as fast as we could for fear the rain should come on and melt the salt. We were then called again to our tasks and worked through the heat of the day; the sun flaming upon our heads like fire and raising salt blisters in those parts which were not completely covered. Our feet and legs, from standing in the salt water for so many hours, soon became full of dreadful boils, which eat down in some cases to the very bone, afflicting the sufferers with great torment. We came home at twelve; ate our corn soup, called blawly, as fast as we could, and went back to our employment till dark at night. We then shovelled up the salt in large heaps, and went down to the sea, where we washed the pickle from our limbs, and cleaned the barrows and shovels from the salt. When we returned to the house, our master gave us each our allowance of raw Indian corn, which we pounded in a mortar and boiled in water for our suppers. We slept in a long shed, divided into narrow slips, like the stalls used for cattle. Boards fixed upon stakes driven into the ground, without mat or covering, were our only beds. On Sundays, after we had washed the salt bags, and done other work required of us, we went into the bush and cut the long soft grass, of which we made trusses for our legs and feet to rest upon, for they were so full of the salt boils that we could get no rest lying upon the bare boards.

Although the United States had banned importation of slavery in 1800, and the UK in 1807, the institution remained firmly entrenched. Mary Prince's account moved so many people, the book sold out three printings in its first year. Little is known about her after the printings other than three lawsuits that were filed as a result of the book. Prince testified at all three. One was brought by the master of the salt ponds, who said he had been defamed. He eventually won.

Prince's narrative was followed by those of such notable women as:

Truth, Sojourner, 1797–1883. *Narrative of Sojourner Truth, a Northern Slave, Emancipated from Bodily Servitude by the State of New York, in 1828.* Edited by Olive Gilbert. Boston: The Author, 1850.

Jacobs, Harriet Ann, 1813–1897. *Incidents in the Life of a Slave Girl. Written by Herself.* Edited by Lydia Maria Child. Boston: The Author, 1861.

Elizabeth, 1766–1866. *Memoir of Old Elizabeth, a Coloured Woman.* Philadelphia: Collins, 1863.

Elizabeth, 1766–1866. *Elizabeth, a Colored Minister of the Gospel, Born in Slavery.* Philadelphia: Tract Association of Friends, 1889.

Dubois, Silvia, 1768–1889. *Silvia Dubois, (now 116 years old): a Biografy of the Slav Who Whipt Her Mistres and Gand Her Fredom.* Edited by Cornelius Wilson Larison. Ringoes, NJ: Larison, 1883.

So we as a race began telling our stories first of bondage, and then of escape.

Brown, Henry Box, 1815–1897. *Narrative of Henry Box Brown, Who Escaped from Slavery Enclosed in a Box 3 Feet Long and 2 Wide. Written from a Statement of Facts Made by*

Himself. With, Remarks upon the Remedy for Slavery. Edited by Charles Stearns. Boston: Brown and Stearns, 1849.

Henson, Josiah, 1789–1883. *The Life of Josiah Henson, Formerly a Slave, Now an Inhabitant of Canada, as Narrated by Himself.* Edited by Samuel A. Eliot. Boston: A. D. Phelps, 1849.

After escape came narratives of freedom:

Keckley, Elizabeth Hobbs, 1818–1907. *Behind the Scenes, or, Thirty Years a Slave and Four Years in the White House.* New York: G. W. Carleton, 1868.

Love, Nat, 1854–1921. *The Life and Adventures of Nat Love, Better Known in the Cattle Country as "Deadwood Dick." By Himself. A True History of Slavery Days, Life on the Great Cattle Ranges and on the Plains of the "Wild and Woolly" West, Based on Facts, and Personal Experiences of the Author.* Los Angeles: The Author, 1907.

So how and where does romance fit into these narratives of telling our own stories?

They begin with the optimism that the race embraced after the Civil War. The abolition of slavery brought not only sweeping change to the three million people who'd been held captive against their will under threat of violence in the South, but changes for a nation that saw a Black governor and lieutenant governor in Louisiana. Integrated legislatures in places like Florida, Mississippi, Georgia, and South Carolina. Two United States senators from Mississippi and twenty-one Black congressmen from all over the South from 1870 to 1901. We as Black people were optimistic about everything from education to owning our own businesses, and the HEA was pursued by formerly enslaved men who spent months and even years walking across the South from plantation to plantation, looking for their wives sold away by slavery. (Even as we still fight the stereotype that our men don't love.) These days also brought hope that the country would live up to the promises stated in the Constitution and that we as a race would get our HEA. But it didn't happen.

When Reconstruction died in 1876, ushering in the hateful, bloody years of Redemption, hope began to falter, but ironically, Black women like Frances Ellen Watkins Harper and Pauline Hopkins held on to that hope and became two of the race's first romance writers. Their stories were based on what scholars called the Victorian love and marriage plots—complete with happy endings. I was surprised to learn that Harper had written one of the earliest romance novels, *Iola Leroy, or Shadows Uplifted*, because she is more remembered for being a poet, lecturer, and fiery speaker for abolition and for suffrage, especially for Black women battling both sexism and racism.

Born free in Maryland in 1825, Frances Ellen Watkins Harper became an orphan at the age of three when both her parents died. She was raised by an aunt and an uncle who was a staunch abolitionist and the founder of the Watkins Academy for Negro Youth, which Frances attended. She published her first book of poetry, *Forest Leaves*, at the age of twenty and, at the age of twenty-six, became the first woman instructor at Union Seminary, a school for free African Americans in Wilberforce, Ohio. When the state of Maryland passed the law forbidding free Blacks' entry into the state, she was unable to return home, and so moved in with Philadelphia's William Still, the famous underground railroad conductor, and his wife, Letitia. Encouraged by the Stills, Frances began writing poetry for anti-slavery newspapers. Her poem "Eliza Harris" was published in William Lloyd Garrison's *The Liberator* and the newspaper *Frederick Douglass' Paper*.

An 1859 letter penned by her to the condemned John Brown, offering her support of him and his wife, was smuggled into his cell. It somehow wound up in the newspapers and was reportedly read by tens of thousands of Americans; it thrust Frances onto the national stage. Also that year, her story "The Two Offers" was published in *The Anglo-African Magazine*, earning her the distinction of being the first Black woman to publish a short story.

For the next decade she traveled across the United States and Canada, speaking out against enslavement on behalf of anti-slavery organizations that had hired her as a traveling lecturer. She also spoke on suffrage. In May 1866, she spoke at the eleventh National Woman's Rights Convention in New York, sharing the stage with Elizabeth Cady Stanton and Susan B. Anthony. Her speech, "We Are All Bound Up Together," touches upon the state of the nation and her desperate attempts to provide for her children after her husband's untimely death. She took white suffragettes to task for their efforts to exclude Black women from the conversations and activism tied to women's rights. The speech is as relevant today as it was then. Reading it gives a good sense of who she was and where she stood. As does this quote from the speech: "I do not believe that white women are dew-drops just exhaled from the skies. I think that like men they may be divided into three classes, the good, the bad, and the indifferent."

In the years after, she would break with Stanton and Anthony over their denunciation of the Fifteenth Amendment, and go on to help found the National Association of Colored Women's Clubs in 1896. She died on February 22, 1911.

Harper is known for many firsts, but her 1858 poem "Bury Me in a Free Land" was as iconic to the pre–Civil War abolition era as "We Shall Overcome" would be for US civil rights. It was read to open and close anti-slavery meetings, was recited at churches and funerals, was tacked on walls of African American homes, and was memorized by African American schoolchildren all over the quasi-free North.

Bury Me in a Free Land

Make me a grave where'er you will,
In a lowly plain, or a lofty hill;
Make it among earth's humblest graves,
But not in a land where men are slaves.

I could not rest if around my grave
I heard the steps of a trembling slave;
His shadow above my silent tomb
Would make it a place of fearful gloom.

I could not rest if I heard the tread
Of a coffle gang to the shambles led,
And the mother's shriek of wild despair
Rise like a curse on the trembling air.

I could not sleep if I saw the lash
Drinking her blood at each fearful gash,
And I saw her babes torn from her breast,
Like trembling doves from their parent nest.

I'd shudder and start if I heard the bay
Of bloodhounds seizing their human prey,
And I heard the captive plead in vain
As they bound afresh his galling chain.

If I saw young girls from their mother's arms
Bartered and sold for their youthful charms,
My eye would flash with a mournful flame,
My death-paled cheek grow red with shame.

I would sleep, dear friends, where bloated might
Can rob no man of his dearest right;
My rest shall be calm in any grave
Where none can call his brother a slave.

I ask no monument, proud and high,
To arrest the gaze of the passers-by;
All that my yearning spirit craves,
Is bury me not in a land of slaves.

Harper's 1892 romance, *Iola Leroy*, has an interesting plot, for the times. Our heroine, Iola, is a light-skinned, blue-eyed woman who doesn't realize she's Black until after the death of her wealthy planter father, when she and her mother are sold into slavery by an unscrupulous relative. Lots of drama ensues. Refusing to pass, she embraces her racial roots and becomes a nurse during the Civil War. She eventually falls in love with a Black doctor. They find their HEA, and both continue to devote their lives to uplifting the race. Dr. Bill Gleason, who teaches English at Princeton and is a romance scholar, says this: "The last paragraph is something like: Now, the shadows were lifted off the hero and heroine, and they're blessed, and can be blessings to each other." Gleason continues, "Harper has a note at the end that basically says: By the way, the mission of this book is to give people faith that this can really happen."

Hope, and an HEA!

The story speaks to race, class, citizenship, gender, and community. According to some reports, the literary critics of the time awarded Harper's 282-page novel more "blame than praise," but it was still continuously reprinted until 1895. After that, it wouldn't see the light of day for over seventy-five years, when it was brought back into print in 1971.

But why would a woman known for her social militancy pen a romance novel at the age of sixty-seven? Was it due to the love she'd found with her husband, who died during their marriage? Had she read Jane Austen's *Pride and Prejudice*, which is embraced as the foundation of modern romance? Toni Morrison famously said if the book you wanted to read isn't in the marketplace, then write it yourself. Was that the reason? Or was Harper simply a romantic at heart, like most romance writers and readers? We'll never know, but the fact that she wrote *Iola Leroy* makes her Black Romance's foundation.

Now, this is 1892. The situation for the race has become more and more dire. Jim Crow is everywhere, Black people are being lynched, disenfranchised, and denied the right to vote. In 1896, the Supreme Court hands down its ruling on *Plessy v. Ferguson*, and by a 7-1 decision makes the Separate but Equal doctrine the law of the land. Yet, in 1900, Pauline Hopkins continues to hold on to the hope and optimism that fueled Harper's *Iola*, and writes a romance called *Contending Forces*. She goes on to write other books in 1901, '02, '03, but each has a tragic ending. Why? Scholar Claudia Tate says in her book *Domestic Allegories of Political Desire*: "Hopkins gave up on romance because the optimism was gone." The race's last hope of an HEA from America was dashed on the rocks of the *Plessy v. Ferguson* ruling, and what little bit of optimism we had dried up like rain in a desert.

Yet our HEAs continued off-page. We were still courted and adored by our men. We married, had children, built the HBCUs (Historically Black Colleges and Universities) because white institutions refused us entry. We founded towns and continued to make as much lemonade as we could out of the lemons America kept giving us.

———

WE SEE MASS market–type romance on-page again in the 1930s, when the widely circulated Black newspaper *The Pitts-*

burgh Courier begins showcasing the Dark Knight, a series about a young Black man from Montana who, after the death of his mother, travels to Chicago and meets the beautiful and wealthy Lyla Durant. After much drama, events, and separations, the two marry and live out their HEA. The series strikes down all manner of stereotypes by showing Black people homesteading in Montana, a man and woman of the race engaging in romantic love, and the wealth held by Black people—especially at a time when the country was more likely to believe the race lived illiterate, impoverished lives.

By the 1950s and '60s, Black romances show up in pulp magazines, but with themes we now categorize as Urban. Mags like *Jive, Copper Romance*, and *Bronze Thrills* featured stories with sensationalized titles like "Lust in My Eyes," "I Flirted with the Wrong Man," "I Was a Call Girl," "No One but a Gangster Wanted Me," and "Who Is My Baby's Father?"

In 1972, Avon Books published *The Flame and the Flower* by Kathleen Woodiwiss, touted as the cornerstone of modern-day romance. With that book, they ushered in an industry that now sells more than all other genre mass market fiction, and puts over a billion dollars a year into publishing's coffers. Black romance readers devoured the subsequent books by Woodiwiss and soon would pick up Rosemary Rogers, Johanna Lindsey, and others, just like their white counterparts—because that was all we had.

The market would change in 1980, when Elsie Washington, an editor at *Newsweek* and the first Black woman to report for *Life* magazine, published *Entwined Destinies* under the pen name Rosalind Welles, for Dell Publishing. It was the nation's first contemporary romance by a Black author. Her editor, a Black woman named Vivian Stephens, would soon move to Harlequin and, in 1984, edit *Adam and Eva* by Sandra Kitt, that publisher's first Black romance writer. *Adam and Eva* and Kitt's *Rites of Spring* are now considered classics of the romance canon. Stephens would also go on to found Romance Writers of America and in 1992 become my first literary agent.

Publishing is only minimally impacted by the debuts of Welles and Kitt, however. In the early 1990s, romance editors are still suggesting that up-and-coming Black romance writers change their characters to white, saying white readers had no desire to read romances with characters that didn't look like them. Marketing divisions are convinced that stories featuring Black couples won't sell because Black people don't read—something a few people in publishing continue to believe to this day. (Never mind the 2014 Pew Research Center report that finds the person most likely to read a book is a college-educated Black woman.) And in the 1990s, a romance editor at a major conference tells a room filled with aspiring Black woman writers that the reason there aren't more Black romances is because Black women just can't write.

Those writers would proceed to walk out en masse.

One of them is now a romance rainmaker for a major house and has published 135 books since her 1995 debut. Her readers of ALL races are glad she didn't allow that editor to kill her dreams.

In response to mainstream publishing's reluctance to open its doors to Black women, Leticia Peoples established Odyssey Books in the early '90s, giving authors like Brenda Jackson, Donna Hill, Rochelle Alers, the late Francis Ray, and others a chance to tell their stories for the first time.

In 1993, forward-thinking Walter Zacharius, president of Kensington Books, makes plans to establish Arabesque, the first imprint targeting the Black romance market. Under the direction of the late, but still beloved, editor Monica Harris, the line debuted in summer 1994 with authors Francis Ray and Sandra Kitt. Black romance readers were ecstatic. Finally, they had books of their own. One reader recalled promptly grabbing a seat in the bookstore and sitting to read there and then. Arabesque soon followed with books by Eboni Snoe, Bette Ford, Carla Fredd, and others.

I also made my historical debut during what is now known as the Summer of Black Love with *Night Song*, published by Avon books. I was harassed into publishing by a work colleague who had just gotten a romance published. I told her about the story I was writing for me. We were working together at a library in Ann Arbor, Michigan. I brought it in. She read it. Encouraged me to get it published. But where? The romance market was closed to us back then. My dream job was to work in a library, so I was good. I had no plans to get published at all! I have no idea how I found Vivian Stephens, but I sent her the manuscript just to shut up my colleague, and she called me less than a week later, offering representation.

Unlike the contemporaries, where multiple authors were making names for themselves, and anthologies like *Rosie's Curl and Weave*, also now considered a classic, you could count on one hand the number of historical romances following *Night Song*. Most notably, *Clara's Promise* by Shirley Hailstock and *Murmur of Rain* by Patricia Vaughn. It would be decades before historicals from authors like Alyssa Cole, Piper Huguley, and Vanessa Riley would arrive on the scene.

Arabesque would eventually be sold to BET, which in turn would sell it to Harlequin. After a few years, Harlequin would discontinue the line.

Yet, Black romance writers refused to give up. Like many other romance authors, they embraced the early rise of e-readers and digital content. Platforms are built, stories once sneered at soar, money is made. And now, thanks to these fearless, savvy writers, Black romance readers are no longer starving for stories that reflect themselves and their lives. The crumbs of before have become a banquet.

So here we are in the twenty-first century, and we've gone from the humble beginnings of *Iola Leroy* to African American women telling their stories in all the subgenres of romance: historical, contemporary, paranormal, and interracial, and via all platforms: indie, traditional, and hybrid. Modern-day romance may trace its roots back to Jane Austen, but there are Frances Ellen Watkins Harper roots, too.

I hope we've made her proud.

Imprint

ALLIE PARKER

My mother taught me to love my skin. Reinforced it daily in ways I never realized until I was much older and away from that constant love. That constant source of reassurance that my skin was beautiful. That I was important. That belief in my words was as strong as any sword. That's the thing about love; when it's constant, you don't know what it feels like to not have it, and when you've never had it, you're not quite sure what you've been missing.

My mother's lessons, like most mothers', never came from nowhere. A particular moment was born of an awkward time when I was about three years old. I grew up in downtown Washington, DC, in a time before most painted it with its current neighborhood name. Now you might call it Logan Circle. At that time, it was noted for its many vices. Drugs. Alcohol. Most notably, sex workers who would stroll certain corners of the neighborhood. To be frank, these activities still occur today, though many pretend they don't.

When I was a little one, the neighborhood sex workers would frequently take their breaks on the park benches around the circle for which the neighborhood was named. It was one of the resting stops that my mother and I would make between our home and the bookstore an exact mile away. A store we frequented. (Another marker in my romantic life, as a corner of that bookstore would be where I would spend hours of my life looking for and reading every romance novel I could discover.)

On this fateful day, when my mother was giving my tiny body a chance to rest among the urban landscape that was my neighborhood, we encountered two women who, while it looked like they had fallen on harder times, were enjoying the afternoon. What can I say? I've always carried an abundance of main character energy, and at that moment in time, I drew their attention. One tried to coax me toward her, but I'd drifted to the other one, almost instinctively.

While I'd toddled off to the other, the one I'd inadvertently snubbed was furious and remarked to my mother what could essentially be translated to "Fuck her, she just hugged a woman riddled with diseases anyway." My mother had dismissed it at the time, and while I myself would like to reflect on it as one of my more Christ-like tendencies, that statement isn't what stuck with her. It was that when she and I returned home not more than ten minutes later, she observed me running directly to my Gem Goldstone doll. I then brought it over to my mom and exclaimed that I'd just met her. That's right, I'd just met the lead singer of the animated rock band Jem and the Holograms.

And Christ-like or not, I—a child who normally displayed an abundance of caution with the closest and kindest relatives— had just hugged a complete stranger because with her pink-streaked blond hair, she had resembled a doll.

That was the moment my mother realized the importance of something we're still attempting to teach today: representation matters. See, the woman I'd snubbed was just as much a stranger and was dressed similarly to the woman I'd instinctually run to; the only difference was that she was Black. My mother had just watched a live-action version of the Clark Doll Experiment.

After the encounter, my mother instituted a policy: I wasn't allowed to have dolls that weren't Black. She couldn't change the makeup of what was in the programs I watched, but the toys coming into our home were going to reflect the image I saw in the mirror.

And so, moving forward in my life, I was never given another white doll. And I, as a child, never even factored the change. It happened and I was.

––––––

I GREW UP in DC. The District of Columbia. Washington, DC. A city that at one point was over 70 percent Black. I never lacked for seeing people who looked like me. Families that looked like mine. Black skin that varied in shades from the deepest dark to fairest of paper white. I often tell people that while I knew I was a minority, I didn't realize I was one until I left home for college, because DC was so heavily majority minority. It was the Chocolate City, after all.

I fell ass-backward into Romance. Most people had the gateway of category books sitting around their grandmother's home or on their mother's nightstand. I didn't. While I came from a family of readers—in fact, my mother, aunt, and grandmother helped found our neighborhood library's "Friends of the Library" group—as far as I could find, the only thing they read were mysteries and the occasional Stephen King. Rarely did anything that seemed like Romance enter our home. That's probably why it took me so long to pick up the copy of *Bridget Jones's Diary* my mother brought home from a book sale one day.

Helen Fielding's seminal chick lit work, while not fully genre romance, hinted at what I felt was missing from my reading life. Every book I gravitated to, that I loved unconditionally, had some element of romance in it. A heroine falling for and kissing a boy that she might not have liked at the beginning of the book or whom she'd been pining for and who surprisingly had been pining for her as well.

It started out simply enough. Back in those days, when Amazon only sold books, books that people curated would be listed alongside the book you were looking at. I'd started there, unsure what I liked exactly, and more and more those lists seemed to lead me to the Romance section in bookstores. So one day I decided to check out a book from the Harlequin category line Blaze, and I was hooked. I read almost every one that I could get my hands on at that bookstore, and at the other three major bookstores I could travel to on my way home from school. And when I ran out of those, I went to the library and checked out every similar book I could find.

Soon I was creating lists of books I needed to find for myself. Backlists to search for. I'd adjusted my routes to and from school so I could check for new books I'd been waiting for to be released on Tuesdays. Knowing that bookstores rotate sections on floors due to sales, I believe that I personally caused the Books-A-Million on Dupont Circle to adjust their floor layout to move the Romance section from the back corner to front and center—right where you were entering the store.

I was no longer reading books. I was consuming Romance, and the moment I'd allowed Romance novels into my life, it was changed.

At first I didn't realize it. I thought I was just happy about the kissing—and let's be honest, the sex—that happened along with jokes and story lines about women deciding to make a change with their lives. Then one day it clicked that no matter how scary things were, no matter how much I might have worried during the dark moment when the hero and the heroine split up, in the end all was well. I got to stop worrying about a happy ending, because that was guaranteed, and when you're fifteen and an awkward, anxiety-riddled Black nerd, that is one of the few guarantees you're given.

Looking back, I realize that I was hyperaware of the dearth of melanin in this genre that I had just fallen deeply in love with. At first I did what I always did when I was growing up; I'd latch on to any slight mention of "olive skin" or "curly hair" or "dusky nipples," and in my mind, all of a sudden this heroine or that hero was suddenly just a super-light-skinned Black person. I'd done it for years when reading kid lit; now wouldn't be different. I was used to not always being represented in the books.

I CAME OF age during the heyday of teenage rom-coms. Say what you will about the John Hughes Brat-Pack era, but the Gen Xers behind the camera in the late 1990s/early 2000s perfected it. If you think I love books, I should tell you about how much I love movies. Movies are a love language in my family. My mother raised me on every movie musical she'd grown up on, and just about every romantic comedy that came out from the 1970s to the present day. In fact, I got a very terse text message that I hadn't told her about *To All the Boys I've Loved Before* when it came out on Netflix.

Loving romantic comedies was part of being able to identify what I loved most about Romance novels. Watching two people fall in love and give in to what they've been fighting for one hour and thirty minutes will never not be my catnip.

The big thing about those movies is that, besides Gabrielle Union, they are extremely white. On top of that, they were full of conventionally attractive people who were given the barest of changes to make them seem like they were outcasts, but I was willing to stomach that wearing glasses and being artsy made you weird and unpopular. That "fat" was a size 8 with full cheeks.

It's rough when you're a teenager and you're a romantic and you wear your heart on your sleeve. How do you sustain the love and confidence you've been given growing up when you're awkward and clumsy and everything you love repeatedly reinforces a specific standard of beauty? When everything you love constantly holds up a single pinnacle of beauty and desire that is absolutely nothing like you? When you worry that you'll never be found desirable because you're constantly shown ways that you're outside the norm?

I had to figure out how to navigate the feelings of unrest that I grew to feel about myself. I didn't have a movie policy like I had a toy policy, and I had to figure it out for myself. Part of what helped me through was genre Romance novels, because with my imagination, I could make these people more like me. It's that simple, right? I'd make these characters fat and Black, because there's no reason they couldn't be. I'd been doing it with the books I'd read as a young kid; what was to stop me from doing it now?

The library, I believe, is the first place I acquired a book by an author who made the heroine out to be something more than skinny. It was a Jennifer Crusie title, which at that point had probably been out for a year or two and which I stumbled onto by accident. Even though the heroine wasn't explicitly fat, she wasn't skinny—and unlike Bridget Jones, she didn't seem to be hell-bent on losing the weight. In fact, she joyfully ate ice-cream bars just like I enjoyed doing. So I started gobbling up everything I could find by Crusie, and used Amazon Lists that included her books to find my way to other books that featured heroines who weren't explicitly skinny—or who were explicitly fat.

———————

I DON'T REMEMBER which list led me to my first Kayla Perrin book, but I remember how I felt purchasing it.

It was spring, and late enough that only the cherry blossoms that grow outside the Tidal Basin were still in bloom. It was the last Friday of the month, which made it a red-letter day, 'cause I not only got my allowance, but any quarter I'd managed to shave off my lunch in the past month was added into my budget.

Also, I was a notorious couch change diver.

What I'm saying is, I'd come prepared to spend a mint.

It was this particular book that intrigued me on my visit that day. In *Say You Need Me*, the heroine was a librarian and, while looking for excitement, had been screwed over by the hero's twin brother in the past. The hero whom the synopsis described as having lips she ached to kiss.

I can't tell you what it was like the moment I looked at that blue cover with brown legs—that resembled my own—in bright red pumps, but it was almost kismet.

I was a teeny bit worried about its delivering the ending I wanted. Though it was in the Romance section, by that time, I had become familiar with the imprints I should see on the spine of a genre Romance novel. I knew of Black category lines, but they weren't always carried in the major bookstores I frequented on a weekly—if not daily—basis. This book didn't feature an

Avon logo on the spine, only HarperCollins. And I was worried it might have been misshelved, but I took a chance anyway.

I didn't know it then, but there were reasons why I had never seen that book in the Romance section at Borders, and reasons why it might have been published with a different imprint. At the time, it didn't matter. I was just very interested in reading about a Black woman who was a librarian and a case of mistaken identity that leads to true love.

As I often did, I started reading the book before I even left the store. That day, rather than walking the easy ten blocks to my house, I waited very patiently at the bus stop for a ride that would easily facilitate my reading. I was willing to risk the wrath of my mother if I wasn't home before her to load the dishwasher.

It was like a light being turned on.

I wouldn't have to adjust in my head that the woman was Black like me and that she was attractive. That she was desired. I couldn't help but tear through it. Soon I was seeking out more books by Perrin, and searching Amazon for lists that comped her book. Books I frequently overlooked started to pop up—books that I had overlooked because they didn't feature the Romance imprint logos I was looking for. The logos that would guarantee for me there would be that main pillar that all Romance readers were looking for. The one that I had only recently discovered as someone new to the genre: a Happily Ever After.

But I found them somehow. I started ordering Arabesque category novels directly when I couldn't find them in the major retailers I frequented. I discovered that a family friend wrote them as well, and I secreted away copies of her novels that were gifted to us. I even once discovered a copy of a western historical romance by Beverly Jenkins that an aunt had bought as an airport read.

Soon I had a new stable of authors to search for on shelves wherever I went. I was no longer just hunting for the next Jennifer Crusie or Susan Andersen. I was also looking for Lynn Emery, Robyn Amos, Rochelle Alers, Brenda Jackson, Francis Ray, and many more.

The beautiful part about being a Romance reader is that it's a big tent with lots of niches that you can plug into at any time and allow yourself to be carried away. And while you may worry for your characters, you know that on the other side of it, they're going to get that HEA. It's freeing and comforting and allows you to lose yourself in their world for a minute because you know, at the end of the day, these characters are loved and will return that love. That people like you are worth rooting for.

IMAGINE IF YOU'VE never seen yourself or someone who looks like you in there. Imagine how that burrows into your psyche and how you go about your life. Imagine if your personhood is constantly up for debate in a genre you love because of the hope it gives everyone else.

Then one day you discover there are books where you do see people who look like you, who are seen as desirable. You're gifted this chance to be Black and happy and carefree. And—even when there's danger—at the end of the book, these characters, these Black women, are going to be safe and cared for and loved. They, like every other Romance character, are worthy of love.

Everyone deserves that, and as a Black woman, that discovery was radical.

It's the doll all over again. Lessons from my mother. Seeing yourself is good for who you are. Loving the skin you're in is the greatest gift that can be given to you.

I'm Rooting for Everybody Black

Black Solidarity, Black World-Building, and Black Love

CAROLE V. BELL

In 2017, at the Emmy red carpet pre-show, a reporter from *Variety* asked internet sensation and creator of the HBO series *Insecure* Issa Rae who she was rooting for to win that night. Rather than single out specific artists, she stated her priorities more broadly: "I'm rooting for everybody Black." With millions watching and tweeting, the statement quickly became a sensation. More important, it stuck. And it transcended internet culture. There were tweets and memes, but also news clips, T-shirts, and sweatshirts, and, perhaps most important, discourse.

Rae's sentiment resonated far and wide. The response was partly because what she said was pithy and concise, the currency of the internet memes. But it also really connected to the social and political climate in that moment (and has ever since). When the concerns of the Black Lives Matter movement are repeatedly met with racial resentment and backlash, a clear public expression of Black solidarity is no throwaway line. Though the killing of George Floyd in 2020 ignited a wave of racial reckoning and recriminations in mainstream publishing, in Black communities nationwide (creative, literary, and general), heightened racial concerns and frustration have long been top of mind, and Black love has long been at least a core part of the answer. The phrase Black Lives Matter first went viral with the acquittal of George Zimmerman for killing Trayvon Martin in 2013 and galvanized into a national movement with protests against police brutality in the wake of the police killing of Michael Brown in Ferguson, Missouri, in 2014. But the phrase has grown to encompass and symbolize a more holistic, renewed demand for Black freedom (at long last), or according to Gene Demby, "the birth of a new Civil Rights Movement."

With increasingly visible demands for justice, though, came renewed pushback. And in 2016, the election of a president with clear ties to white nationalists only made the need for a reprieve from injustice more pressing and real. As revanchist white supremacy and racial resentment have become more publicly bold and omnipresent, the thirst—in truth, the heartfelt visceral and pressing need—for cultural experiences of Black joy and Black love as a reprieve from all that only grows stronger. As Hanif Abdurraqib writes in his recent essay collection, *A Little Devil in America*, Black culture has long been an essential element in how Black Americans have coped with pain. In the seventies, Abdurraqib contends, soul music allowed Black people to be "their whole free selves" and the joy found within that was essential: "A people cannot only see themselves suffering, lest they believe themselves only worthy of pain, or only celebrated when that pain is overcome."

I felt that. Outside of music, in the literary arts, no medium and no single genre expresses that particular irrepressible need to see one's self—one's whole, lovable, soft human self—on a more instinctual, elemental level than Black romance. For many African American readers, the 2010s saw Black romance as an answer to a new racial reckoning, in an intimate and visceral way. The reasons for this are many. Romance is known as the literature of hope for all readers, but for Black readers navigating a world that discounts the value of Black life and denies the existence of Black humanity, Black beauty, and Black people's capacity for love, the idea of romance as hope has additional weight. That's especially true in times of elevated external stress and obvious strife. On-screen, we have *Sylvie's Love* and *Lovers Rock*. In literature we have Black romance novels, not just books by authors about Black people finding love, but rather stories specifically by Black people about Black people finding love with each other.

While mainstream publishing looks for racial redemption in interracial romance and multicultural stories about transcending race, my yearslong deep dive into Black romance has affirmed one central truth: for many Black readers and authors, freedom and happiness can be found through the embrace of Black love that is inextricably bound up with Black solidarity. To be clear, "love is love." But even as interracial marriages grow increasingly common in the United States, and multiculturalism and diversity are ostensibly core American values, there is a strong sense that nothing provides a greater feeling of security and emotional fulfillment than Black unity and solidarity. One of the boldest statements artists can make is Black solidarity and joy over oppression and pain. One of the most resonant ways that Black writers express self-love and find joy is in stories about Black love.

The Link between Love and Justice in Romance

There are two dominant ways that Black love stories speak to Black readers under stress and striving for freedom. First, some Black romance confronts racism and the struggle for Black liberation head-on. As African American literary scholar Rita Dandridge has shown, from its inception, Black romance has also had a strong social realist and activist bent running through it, reminding ourselves and others of the fullness of our lives as well as our struggles. Black women are "agents of resistance" in these romances, but they also find love. We see that in the work of Frances Harper and in the historical romances published starting in the 1990s by Beverly Jenkins and others.

That activist streak shows up in Black historical and contemporary romance today. The activist-minded protagonist is a beloved romance archetype. The anthology *Daughters of a Nation*, for example, is a collection of stories about Black women in the fight for suffrage. Writing for *O, The Oprah Magazine*, Alyssa Cole called attention to the political concerns in her 2020 Runaway Royals novel: "While it's set in a fictional kingdom, *How to Catch a Queen*, like so many romance novels, was clearly shaped by the politics of the world around me and—specifically, America today." Cole has also made explicit connections between justice and joy in her Loyal League historical romance series about Black spies working undercover for the Union during the Civil War.

But Black romance also serves as escape and reprieve from the ongoing struggle for Black liberation—a place of refuge and fantasy and a way of finding Black joy that isn't always accessible elsewhere. Plus, as historian Nicole Jackson argues, merely focusing on Black love has, historically, often been an act of rebellion. Romance is arguably the genre that most consistently celebrates the fullness of Black life, and is where many readers have looked to find refuge from the burden of racism and rediscover Black joy separate from its struggles. I feel that, and I see that sentiment reflected all around me in reviews, on social media, through Black bloggers and authors. Book blogger/YouTuber Shade Lapite of the *Coffee BookShelves* blog likened discovering Tia Williams's rom-com *The Perfect Find* to finding water in the desert, but lamented not having more books like it in romance and other genres: "If there's a group of people that deserve uplifting, joyful, life-affirming art, surely it's Black people. Where is it?"

This is not to say that romance is ever purely apolitical. I strongly believe that who is centered and what a happily ever after looks like have political implications, and bringing to life a more just world on the page can be as political as delineating what makes this world unjust. Plus, like Cole and others, I understand that ideas about beauty and desirability have racial and political dimensions. As cultural scholars have long argued, desire is not born solely of individual preference, no matter what we may want to believe. It is shaped by and reflected in culture, social hierarchies, and social conventions that help dictate which physical characteristics are highly valued and which are not. Context matters. Even the least explicitly political romance novels manifest these ideas about beauty and worth, and they can also contest them. Some novels do so subtly, by putting on the page a vision of love in which Black celebration and joy far outweighs any burden, and racism is unlikely to be a pressing concern.

This essay explores how those two impulses—the confrontation of injustice and escape from it—have played out in an emphasis on Black solidarity as a conduit for Black Freedom and in the construction of extensive Black Community and even Black Worlds within the work of three leading authors of Black romance in the six years since the incidents that sparked the rise of the new civil rights struggle, the Movement for Black Lives.

Researching Black Love

In the midst of increasingly visible racial injustice in the United States and the resurgent grassroots activism of Black Lives Matter (BLM), it's inevitable for this energy to increasingly find its way onto the page in some way. And it's also inevitable for modern Black romance to have to navigate and find a way to reconcile those two impulses—the drive toward justice and the need for joy. The question is how. How has the Black romance community in America responded to and engaged with the values and ideas about identity and justice reflected in the Black Lives Matter movement?

More specifically, I've long wanted to know: How are Black romance authors channeling their concerns and anxieties about racial injustice onto the page? Is it by directly interrogating racial justice through plot lines involving social justice, or in other ways— by insulating readers from the injustices and ensconcing them in visions of what the "good life," a more just life, could look like beyond white supremacy's reach? If and when Black romance authors do engage with racial justice on the page, which ideologies of race do they convey implicitly or explicitly in the texts? To answer these questions, I examined some of the most popular and often-discussed Black romance. First, I identified dozens of notable Black romances of the last six years based on ratings and reviews on Goodreads and Black blogs.

Looking at the six-year period beginning in 2015, I found that some of the most consistently beloved and widely read Black romances were those authored by Alexandria House, Christina C. Jones, and Alyssa Cole—writers who engage in discussions of racial justice in a variety of ways that range from subtle/implicit to explicit. These three authors consistently support their Happily Ever Afters by wrapping their couples in Black communities of support and by engaging in the kind of sophisticated world-building that spans series as well as individual books. So, while Black romances often hinge on universally popular tropes like fake dating, fated mates, friends to lovers, enemies to lovers, and second chances, many authors take these universal tropes and make them new by grounding them in culturally specific

Black experience. Situated in predominantly Black contexts, the world-building around Black community and institutions can be just as essential to these stories as the romantic trope. By ensconcing their characters in Black worlds—not just tight-knit Black family and friend groups (though those are essential) but also environments in which happiness and safety are secured through predominantly Black institutions, Black businesses, Black communities, and Black political power—they help to blunt the reach and impact of white supremacy. In fact, the pull of Black community is so strong, so central to the well-being of Black people in these books, that when Alyssa Cole wrote her first novel outside the romance genre, the gentrification thriller *When No One Is Watching*, she centered her story on the polar opposite of Black safe space, a historic Black neighborhood under attack.

Still, these books don't just idealize a Black utopia in the absence of white folks on the page. They both long for and reckon with justice within Black communities as well. That is to say, the vision of justice on the page is often noticeably intersectional. Concerns about class, color, and gender roles, for example, often loom large. And social issues sometimes play a big role. In a way, freeing these communities from the relentless concern about racism frees them up to focus on dealing with issues within.

In *The Devil You Know: A Black Power Manifesto*, Charles Blow argues much the same. Believing that chasing acceptance in white-dominant worlds to be a losing proposition, Blow contends that Black people could best mitigate the harms of white supremacy by reversing the Great Migration. His advice: those who have the flexibility to do so should turn their backs on the North and reclaim population majorities and power in the South.

As both an avid reader of romance and an academic specializing in media and politics, I was struck by how much Charles Blow's vision resembled what I was already seeing on the pages of some of the most popular Black romances. The Black majority communities and businesses and institutions Blow dreams of in his manifesto vividly come to life in the fictional worlds of writers like Alexandria House and Christina C. Jones, and—transferred to a fictional African nation just as in *Black Panther*—Alyssa Cole. Though their aims and styles differ, much of the vision is the same. Decenter whiteness; reclaim Black solidarity, Black Power. Black Freedom. All this can be located through an expansive application of Black love.

These ideas about Black love, freedom, and solidarity are perhaps most clearly expressed in some of the most popular works by three prominent Black romance authors: The McClain Brothers and Romey University series by Alexandria House, The Love Sisters series by Christina C. Jones, and the Reluctant Royals and Runaway Royals series by Alyssa Cole. In this essay, I use examples from books in these series—specifically Alyssa Cole's *How to Catch a Queen*, Alexandria House's *Let Me Free You*, and Christina C. Jones's *I Think I Might Love You*—to provide insights into the multitude of ways that ideas about Black freedom and Black solidarity are bound together with representations of

Black love, all intrinsic elements in the HEA within Black romance.

I chose these books specifically after two years of my own journey into reading Black romance. Once I started to research Black romance in a more focused way, I looked for books that were both widely read and highly respected/rated within Black romance communities. I identified potential titles using the "Black Romance" or "African American Romance" tags on Goodreads, lists, and the Sistah Girls and Women of Color in Romance websites, as well as a variety of Black romance blogs. And I also looked for titles with 1,000 total ratings and a 3.5 or higher average reader rating to ensure the titles I identified were embraced and discussed within the Black romance community. These themes of Black solidarity and community emerged throughout, across many dozens of works in myriad subgenres. But the books I eventually chose to focus on here stand out for their clear vision of what a good and just life looks like and/or for protagonists who are engaged with social justice themselves.

What This Black Love HEA Looks Like on the Page

In the works of House, Jones, and Cole, these underlying themes of Black solidarity, liberation, and power show up as intrinsic elements in living Happily Ever After in Black love. That manifests most concretely in: how financial security is attained; dependence on Black economic self-determination; Black community and institutions; a reverence for Black aesthetics/beauty independent of European ideals; and in Black power. All three novels also take an intersectional view of justice that acknowledges that oppression has many forms, and justice is not accomplished just by neutralizing white supremacy alone, but also by attending to social problems within Black communities.

Black Beauty, Black Spaces, and Economic Self-Determination in *Let Me Free You*

Let Me Free You, a soapy dramedy about a green-card marriage, is the highest-rated novel in House's McClain Brothers series (4.73 stars out of 5 on Goodreads). It manages to be supremely romantic, tropey, and overtly political all at the same time. It takes place in predominantly Black spaces; interrogates the standards of Black femininity, questioning the internal social hierarchies of class, color, and desirability that still hold sway in Black communities; boldly confronts a controversial archetype of modern Black masculinity; and includes a brief but explicit discussion of the influence of white supremacy in American culture.

Neil McClain and Sage Moniba are both a bit bruised by life and love. Neil has never lacked female company. He's conventionally handsome and comes from a tight-knit working-class family that has attained a significant level of wealth because of the professional success of Neil's three brothers: one a rapper, another a professional athlete, and the third a businessman. Sage is a good girl and a good friend to the women in Neil's closest circle, including his eldest brother's wife. She is also a successful makeup artist with a growing clientele. Neil is a college-educated writer, artist, and bookstore owner, but he's also recently out of rehab and feeling kind of shaky. When Sage is threatened with deportation, their friends come up with the idea of a green-card marriage, an arrangement to help Sage stay in the country she's called home since she was a small child. Sage gets to stay and Neil gets to do something good and pay forward some of the goodwill and good fortune from which he's benefited.

Despite the nature of the arrangement, however, it soon becomes clear that Neil and Sage are supremely well suited to bringing out the best in each other. Neil has struggled with substance abuse and self-worth, and he's known somewhat pejoratively as a screwup and as "Hotep Neil." He's the sensitive and intellectual brother, the one most concerned about culture, Black identity, and race. Sage is darker skinned, short and big with a big laugh, big personality, and an infamously loud voice. And she doesn't possess the external validations of success that some would expect Neil's partner to have. Neil initially recalls her as "The little thick one? Loud as hell?" To be clear: none of that bothers him, but he's not keen on marrying a stranger. Sage has endured more than her fair share of verbal abuse and denigration by other Black women and sexual partners, which makes her vulnerable to manipulation that plays on her insecurities. They both feel like underdogs and they're attracted to each other intellectually and physically. And yet, according to some of the secondary characters, especially their exes, their coupling is anything but natural. Some people in their circle communicate the idea that Sage is unworthy of Neil's attention and love because of her darker complexion and her larger size, both qualities which place her outside the standards for a good-looking, well-off, and well-connected Black man. That Sage is stable and Neil has struggled with substance abuse does little to lessen his worth on the dating market according to some hierarchies, even within some Black communities.

The fact that Neil and Sage get on like a house on fire and are simultaneously perfectly matched and considered an unlikely couple according to social standards becomes the best argument for questioning the legitimacy of those standards. Unlikely couples like this—ones who are perfect for each other but flout social convention and endure social sanction—wield symbolic power. These portrayals are potent vehicles of social criticism. In this case, Neil's devotion and passion resoundingly call into question the validity of the intra-community biases around class and color.

Portrayals of characters who defy conventional standards don't always need to be contested on the page. I've written before that it's important to just have these characters of size be cherished without having them go through the shaming. But House's handling is effective and her portrait of Sage has real depth. House isn't the only author to represent a character like Sage, but she's doing something with this story line that is effective and heart-wrenching, and she makes Sage a unique and striking figure. Sage is someone whose voice and personality receive as much censure as her size. It speaks to the constricting standards imposed on women, Black women especially, who are often told they don't fit the feminine ideal. That's a phenomenon many Black women recognize. What's also lovely is that Neil fully embraces Sage. Their chemistry is palpable, and social pressure doesn't make him question his choice. But those pressures do lead Sage to question his sincerity. It also makes them targets of jealousy and resentment and harassment by their exes. Their HEA directly hinges upon not simply rejecting those problematic and false standards (some of which are direct holdovers from white supremacy), but really working through them as a lie about Neil's reason for staying in the marriage brings both main characters to a literal precipice in the book's dramatic climax.

Although questions about the relationship between beauty and Blackness are of particular importance to Sage in *Let Me Free You*, since she both withstands criticism for her looks and works in the beauty industry, these issues are implicitly the subtext of a wide range of Black romances. One of the many reasons Black romance is a safe space is that, aesthetically and culturally, these novels have a commitment to the beauty and culture of people of African descent. Natural hairstyles from afros to locs and braids are all common, styles that are recognized initially as Afrocentric. They find beauty in a Black woman's body with thick thighs and full hips, in dark skin, in faces with broad features. Traits treated as flaws by Eurocentric American standards, those most often associated with Blackness, and hairstyles that might be banned in corporate and government environments, are celebrated in Black romance. Conversely, people who don't have an appreciation for Black beauty, those who practice colorism and feature and size discrimination, are misguided and suspect at least, and antagonists in thrall to internalized white supremacy at worst, like Neil's ex-girlfriend and Sage's boyfriend. Frequently, that kind of destructive attitude goes along with some broader villainy, as is seen here.

Black Entrepreneurship as Liberation

Economic independence is another key part of the HEA for Black protagonists in *Let Me Free You*. Sage and Neil's HEA is also tied up in their lives as Black business owners catering to Black clientele. Neil owns an Afrocentric bookstore. This aspect of Neil's backstory combines the freedom of entrepreneurship with his interest in both Afrocentrism and Black liberation. One of the ways Sage and Neil bond is by sharing and discussing books. Sage hasn't had the formal educational opportunities Neil has had, but they read and discuss books together.

Freeing oneself from the compromises involved in working for a white institution is a key part of the heroine's struggle and journey to happiness in many Black romances, including *I Think I Might Love You* by Christina C. Jones as well as *Let Me Free You*. Protagonists often end up as entrepreneurs who cater primarily to a Black clientele. That means freedom from a boss but also freedom from white judgment. This theme also appears in *Let Me Love You* by Alexandria House, book one of House's Mc-Clain Brothers series, though that's the beginning of her journey. By the end, Jo Walker controls her own fate. She ends up married to Everett McClain, a major recording artist who controls his fate by producing his own records, running not just his own record company but also, eventually, an entertainment company. To be fair, achieving self-determination and financial independence are often part of the character arc in romance. And problematic white supervisors or employers and white power structures are a source of struggle in interracial romances like *Sweet Tea* by Piper Huguley, too. But the employers and businesses that are part of the HEA in Black romance tend to have a race-conscious aspect, more consistently falling under the heading of "for us, by us."

Afrocentricity and White Supremacy

Even though Alexandria House locates Neil and Sage within Black community and Black entrepreneurship, and even though she also surrounds Neil and Sage with a fair amount of insulation, which allows many Black romance novels to take the focus off of whiteness and white people, she makes a conscious choice to confront the controversy in Black culture around how the spectre of white supremacy haunts Black people's judgment of each other. Sage, who is originally from Liberia, is a target for that particular brand of toxicity derived from internalized European norms. Plus, by making the male protagonist a supposedly infamous hotep, House calls into question what being a hotep really means and why so many Black people hold the idea in such contempt when its core value is Afrocentrism. The figure of the hotep has come to signify not pride in Black identity and African cultural affinity, but rather a parody of it, according to Damon Young, writing for *The Root* ("Hotep, Explained"). In addition to questions about gender roles, Neil's reputation as a hotep leads Sage to ask not just "Why are you a hotep?" but also "Why you hate white people?"

Neil's response has two pieces. First, he points to the centrality of white supremacy in American culture and education:

"Well, because ever since I was little, I didn't understand why everything we learned was so . . . white. We're taught that classical music is white, classical art is white, classical dance is ballet— white. All the great thinkers—white . . . I just ain't never bought into that Eurocentric bullshit."

Second, he draws a clear line:

"I don't hate white people, I hate white supremacy. I hate white lies and not the innocent lies they label as white lies. You see how perverse that shit is? A white lie is an innocent lie? What the fuck is an innocent lie? That shit don't exist. But that's what they do . . . they make stuff benefit them."

Given who Neil is, an intellectual and a generous and devoted husband, putting those words in his mouth makes a powerful statement. *Let Me Free You* is brilliantly titled because in the end, Neil and Sage rescue and free each other emotionally and intellectually. They find not just love, but freedom. The title and their journey as a couple reminded me of a line I knew from Bob Marley's "Redemption Song," but which originated in a

1937 speech by Marcus Garvey: "Emancipate yourself from mental slavery. None but ourselves can free our minds." Neil would approve.

Black Power and Social Justice in Alyssa Cole's *How to Catch a Queen*

Black community, world-building, and debates about social equality and the legacy of white rule play an even greater role in *How to Catch a Queen*. Alyssa Cole's boldly, intersectionally feminist novel takes place in a world apart from Sage and Neil, in the tiny fictional African nation of Njaza. Following the success of her award-winning Reluctant Royals series, in 2020 Alyssa Cole launched the Runaway Royals with a romance about a temporary and volatile arranged marriage of convenience between two people who, unlike Neil and Sage, are near polar opposites emotionally and do not easily mesh.

King Sanyu II was born to lead his small African kingdom. Shanti Mohapti is a former farm girl from a neighboring nation; she has great ambition but no pedigree. And yet, defying both fictional and reader expectations about gender and class, between these two, Shanti Mohapti is the natural-born alpha. Sanyu has major doubts about whether he wants that life or is even suited to it. So he mostly leaves the decision-making to his advisers, and when the novel opens, he's a few steps from fleeing the throne. While King Sanyu II fights chronic, almost debilitating anxiety daily, and secretly dreams about finding true love, Shanti spends her time dreaming of and planning national leadership. Plus, she has confidence, experience, and political savvy to spare. Shanti not only believes with unshaking certainty, against all odds given her humble roots, that she was born to be a queen; she has worked to make that dream a reality. She studied relevant subjects at university and identified potential matches—countries in need of a female monarch for their single king.

No one inside Njaza's palace expects this pairing to last, much less for a love match to grow between a man who was born to be king but doubts his own fitness to rule and a woman who has craved and planned for power her whole life. The match only comes about out of desperation. Sanyu's father is dying and wants to see his son settled before he goes. Shanti, meanwhile, has struggled to find a home. Despite beauty and many qualifications, her lack of pedigree rules her out as a desirable match for most monarchs. Timing is everything, though, and Njaza lacks the time to find someone else. So in addition to differences in temperament, the hasty, slapdash nature of their match creates distance between the two potential lovers.

How Cole Puts Politics in the Spotlight

While genre conventions place Shanti and Sanyu's romantic relationship at the center of the story, Cole puts their political partnership and Shanti's secret political activism on equal footing with their romantic coupling. To be clear, this queen can do both. Shanti is a beautiful woman, thirsty for companionship and bursting with ambition. Among the many feminist elements in the novel, Shanti's unabashed desire to lead and to do so by starting at the top as a monarch is among the boldest. That type of ambition isn't often a quality we see praised in women. But Cole makes it clear that any kingdom would be lucky to have her. Shanti is, we are told, one of "University of Thesolo's most valued students, having completed degrees and certifications in multiple disciplines to prepare for the eventuality of taking a throne—and, truth be told, for the slim possibility that she wouldn't, because a queen always has a contingency plan." And she arrives in Njaza armed with big dreams and a binder full of research and strategic plans. Personally and professionally, with her beauty, openness, education, confidence, and political savvy, she is the partner Sanyu needs to break out of his protective shell and move his country forward.

Nonetheless, their road to partnership is far from easy and that struggle is what makes *How to Catch a Queen* such an explicitly political novel. Cole places Shanti and Sanyu's journey toward a multifaceted romantic partnership and the country's journey toward gender and social justice hand in hand. One cannot succeed without the other. In Njaza, Shanti finds herself immersed in a deeply unequal and rigidly sexist system uninterested in her talent or her plans. Shanti is truly sidelined, excluded from taking part in her new country's governance, both substantively and ceremonially. This isn't, contrary to her expectation, an opportunity to lead or show what she can do. It's an invitation to go through the motions of a temporary, sort of probationary marriage in which she's never supposed to succeed, or even play the role of temporary figurehead.

After months with little contact between them, a candid conversation exposes the gap between Shanti's hopes and reality. Shanti is not just disappointed. She's bewildered by how marginalized she's been:

> *"We've barely spoken since the wedding. You've paid less attention to me than a pet hermit crab. You haven't checked on my comfort or even if my water bowl was filled! You haven't included me in any aspect of the running of the kingdom either."*
>
> *He stopped and looked down at her. "Why would I include you in running the kingdom?" he asked, completely straight-faced.*

Despite having grown up in neighboring nations, culturally they're worlds apart. Shanti came of age in a kingdom in which the king and queen ruled "together," as partners:

> *"They're a team, each having their strengths and weaknesses, and their advisors and ministers support that team—in political matters, that is. It's hard for a person to run a kingdom on their own because one person never has all the answers.*
>
> *"I thought you and I might be a good match because I want to help your kingdom and I assumed you did, too, and that's more of a shared interest than many arranged marriages have. And I thought the choice of me as your bride had been strategic because you wanted to forge ties with Thesolo."*

Sanyu's words and his expression reveal how foreign that notion is to him: "I had no choice in you as a bride, and I doubt your connection to Thesolo was taken into account," he says. "You were likely chosen for your looks." And yet, she thinks, ironically, she's "not even allowed to be arm candy."

In contrast with Shanti, who had both her parents' marriage and the egalitarian monarchy to look up to, Sanyu was explicitly raised not to believe in love, or to trust, or to think that a woman could be his true partner, let alone that they could work together as equals. He grew up without a mother, seeing a parade of temporary queens pass through the palace, never staying long enough to really bond. Time and again, "He'd been reminded every time he'd been told his mother was gone because she hadn't been strong enough or smart enough or cunning enough— or docile enough or sweet enough . . ." Between this talk and archival research into her new home, Shanti realizes that Sanyu's upbringing, his maternal abandonment, and his socialization by male elders (especially a domineering, very old-school senior advisor, Musoke) have made gender equality, the egalitarian model of marriage as partnership, and even love completely foreign concepts: "She thought about Musoke, and his rigid point of view. Of a little boy who watched queen after queen arrive and be sent away, and what kind of man that boy might become."

As their conversation illustrates, despite growing up in neighboring countries, Shanti and Sanyu's differences—not just in temperament but in ideology, culture, and family upbringing— are stark. He obviously doesn't understand a woman like Shanti, let alone know how to work alongside and love her. Between his upbringing, her identity as an outsider and a woman, and the jockeying for power among different factions working against them, her plans for partnership appear almost impossible. But this Black romance is a literature of hope and change. Sanyu is willing to learn. Eventually, it's something they both fight to make real.

How Intersectional Politics and Social Justice Fit in a Fairy Tale

Culture and ideology also play a central role in the story. *How to Catch a Queen* is a beautiful distillation of the way culture and politics intersect and the importance of taking an intersectional view of social justice. Njaza is an African country. Black leadership dominates at every level. And they are proud of their heritage, in particular their defeat of European colonial rule. But that doesn't eliminate injustice in the nation. So while there are definitely fairy tale–like elements in the commoner who married royalty, it's also a story that's mostly interested in belief systems, political realities, and models of change. Cole herself disclosed that Sanyu and Shanti's happily ever after could not have come about without their working to make their world more just: "The 'happily ever after' comes only after Shanti and her king, Sanyu, navigate toxic masculinity, a government made of old men who refuse to respect fresh ideas from younger generations, and a community of marginalized people who organize in the back of a bookstore to help drag their country into the future."

Fortunately, Cole excels at distilling real-world politics into story and myth. *How to Catch a Queen* very effectively examines how culture and belief systems function and how change is sometimes made. Njaza is a young country whose cultural identity is largely focused on their story of independence from colonial rule. Unfortunately, Njazan leaders use that origin story to justify their biases and privilege. Following its independence, after a brief democratic experiment, Njaza has been ruled by two men, revolutionary warriors and founding fathers: a king, who was Sanyu's father, and his closest adviser, Musoke. Democracy, the story goes, was contentious and messy: "They tried that. And it led to civil war."

Cole also cleverly gives the country an origin story about a missing queen that, somewhat like the biblical story of Adam and Eve's banishment from the Garden of Eden, blames a female ancestor for an entire culture's deeply ingrained sexism and misogyny. Though the story sounds like a myth because it's dressed in tales of heroic soldiers and kingdoms, Cole is really modeling how ideologies truly function in society. She has given the kingdom of Njaza a controlling image of women, an ideologically driven stereotype that provides justification for the existing social relations. Controlling images, according to sociologist and leading Black feminist Patricia Hill Collins, provide cover, making it seem that the way things are is how they should be.

Njaza's origin story also makes loving a woman a weakness. This (in addition to anxiety) is why Sanyu spends the first three months of their planned four-month trial marriage almost completely avoiding his wife.

Cole also addresses how the governing structure of Njaza

reinforces social inequality. After a disastrous public appearance in which he's heckled and experiences a bout of anxiety, Shanti passes Sanyu a response to a question posed by a member of the public, which he later contemplates in bed: "How can women and other marginalized genders feel like full citizens when we have no voice in this kingdom?" Just beneath that is a handwritten quote:

> *If a troop of lions gather to make the rules of the land, they will agree that eating antelopes and aardvarks is in the best interest of everyone. If a group of lions, antelopes, and aardvarks gather to make the rules of the land, the final decision will look very different, don't you think? —Queen Ramatla of Thesolo*

Despite the fictional setting, Cole's depiction of the connections between politics, identity, and ideology, and the wary relationship between former colonies and their colonizers, are spot on.

Finding Community

Ultimately, finding a community for herself outside the palace walls is an essential part of Shanti's journey. Neglected, restless, and bored, Shanti decides to explore Njaza on her own at night and stumbles upon a whole community inside the aptly named Liberation Bookstore. Not just potential new friends but progressive like minds and an outlet for her prodigious talent and energy. The bookstore gives Shanti a window into the Njazan people's point of view and their frustrations—on gender and patriarchy, for example:

> "I'd hoped the queen would bring Ingoka's fire to us, to smite Omakuumi and his cult of strength and Amageez and his logic that makes no sense," she said as she stacked papers. "It's such silliness! As if to be fierce and intelligent, one must be born male."
>
> "Or as if you should crush your true self to retain Omakuumi's blessing or Amgeez's," Salli said. "I sometimes still feel guilty, but my husband and wife remind me that I am their blessing, and that all of this stuff they say to make us feel bad about ourselves isn't the true way of Njaza."

Here Salli alludes to the idea that a more fluid vision of gender and sexuality is part of true Njazan culture suppressed under colonialism. Sanyu's best friend and adviser, Lumu, is also in a triad with a husband and wife. Yet, it's also clear that internalized holdovers from European rule are only part of the problem. Njazan founders forged their own traditions and myths in independence. That includes the myth of the True Queen, which turned the king's wife into a legendary figure, a standard no human woman ever seems to meet, and the ritual of the marriage trial, which never succeeds. Time and again, "Somehow, none of the wives had managed to fit the role." Here again the intersection between identity and ideology emerges. At the bookstore, Marie, an elder, exposes the ideal of the True Queen for what it is: convenient justification for gender inequality, a reason no woman is ever fit. The myth robs women at the top of the social ladder of opportunity to lead, and that devaluation flows to those many rungs down:

> *"These decisions that seem wasteful to us always benefit someone. A queen without power who can be replaced at any time," she said darkly, then shook her head.*
>
> *"Whatever the initial reason for it, it lets every woman in Njaza now know her place. If the most important woman in the land is little more than a temporary trinket—not even a trophy, which is shown off—then the seamstress and shop owner and the shepherdess shouldn't expect any better."*

Though technically an insider, and despite enjoying the trappings of privilege in theory, both because of Njazan culture and because of the nature of her marriage, Shanti is marginalized. So she finds her own community, a refuge and a safe space, outside of it. Among activists at the bookstore, Shanti finds her purpose, putting her political education and energy into helping those who are powerless in Njaza to build a political movement, to agitate and bring pressure for change from the outside. She mentors the protestors, sharing information about effective methods of public confrontation in a place like Njaza that hasn't had a culture of protest for fifty years. And Shanti and the activists' efforts bear fruit. Soon "the streets are full of debate about what the king is doing for us, and why some of us are said to be equal when paying taxes but don't get to determine how the tax money is used." Plus, "people no longer feel a need to whisper their complaints." For once, Shanti sees the success and gets the credit she is due, for her contributions and ideas and for sharing vital information about activism around the world.

Still, it's an odd position to be in, playing both the outside and inside game, and Shanti has mixed feelings when credited with the success of events that cast Sanyu in a critical light: "It felt like treason now, to hear Sanyu spoken of this way and not defend him, but Marie and the others had every right to be angry." Even worse, when the activists get creative, remixing a patriotic anthem into protest rap, Shanti is more ambivalent than triumphant, "proud of her friends, but wondering what it meant that a queen was complicit in the heckling of her king." She's especially reticent about calls for insurrection, attempting to defuse the more bloodthirsty radicals' not entirely metaphorical cheers for the guillotine and to make things go "Boom." Her goal, she thinks, "was to prevent it, not stoke the flames."

Ultimately, community is central to how Shanti and Sanyu finally find their way forward. Once Shanti and Sanyu start to work together and become lovers, they collaborate on a raft of proposals for economic development and equality. But he's plagued by worry and torn between his old adviser and tradition and Shanti's drive for progress. So, at the last moment, without warning Shanti, Sanyu drops the equality aspect of their plans in front of the council, fearing it's a step too far that might jeopardize other initiatives. His betrayal pushes Shanti out of the palace and on the run. Shanti discovers a community of former Njazan queens, who tell her the nation's true history and the role the first queen played in independence. Shanti and Sanyu's reconciliation and their HEA then essentially hinge on Shanti bringing the missing pieces of Njazan history, the parts involving women specifically, to light. Those stories help Sanyu understand his personal history as well as the country's past. They become the basis of a restorative justice project that Shanti leads, one that will form the basis for transforming Njaza and ensuring that it has a more inclusive future. Other types of community, close friends, and Shanti's community of activists in particular, play essential roles in their love story. But it's the support and guidance of those elder women that help Shanti and Sanyu make the final leap from estranged lovers to permanent and true partners.

The Lighter Side of Black Solidarity in *I Think I Might Love You*

While *Let Me Free You* and *How to Catch a Queen* reflect the richness and depth of the ideas manifested in Black romance, they occupy the more explicit, serious side of the spectrum in terms of how ideas about a just and good life are communicated in Black romance. Christina C. Jones's *I Think I Might Love You*, on the other hand, demonstrates how ideas about Black solidarity are subtly manifested at the lighter side of the spectrum, within romantic comedy. Jones's novella is a great and subtle representation of solidarity, Black power, and the corrosiveness of internecine conflicts about class.

In fact, despite savvy and subtle commentary on ingroup respectability politics and Black solidarity and, in its own way,

Black power, *I Think I Might Love You* is the funniest novella I've ever read. The story begins with a meet disaster—after a category 5 breakup involving a cheating man and an angry wife, Jaclyn Love seeks shelter in what she thinks is her sister's empty apartment, only to find a naked man there whom she attacks. She thinks she's defending herself against an intruder when the man is really her sister's subletter. The tenant, Kadan Davenport, is a hot animal doc. Jaclyn's a kind of hotheaded woman who's already had a run-in or two with the law.

When we first meet her, at the door of the apartment fumbling for her keys, Jac's twerking her worries away and rapping along to an angry song on the night she finds out her live-in boyfriend is actually married. Her attitude, captured in the music, the dance, and the thought, "Oh well. One fuckboy don't stop this show," reflect admirable resilience. Unfortunately, her irrepressibility and an indomitable spirit are also captured on surveillance cameras when she takes her anger out on the ex-boyfriend's very expensive car:

> *Surveillance, from the parking garage. With audio. The tires were already flat, and the brick was already through the window. But there I was, locs swinging, rapping "Wrong Bitch" at the top of my lungs while I spray-painted those same words on the hood of Victor's precious black Mercedes.*

The penalty Jaclyn receives is harsh: "Four hundred hours of community service. That was the price to be paid for my drunken shenanigans with Victor's car. Carrie Underwood and Jazmine

Sullivan had me out here bad." We learn two things from Jac's run-in with the law. First, this is not Jac's first encounter with the legal system: "The judge had given me a specific list of places where I could fulfill my service hours, and I was not trying to end up raking leaves at the park, or picking up trash off the side of the road. I'd already done both of those." Second, despite the extensive community service, it's also clear that Blakewood is a place where a volatile young Black woman can get into a little trouble and not lose her life or her livelihood. But it's not so welcoming and supportive that a strict Black judge can't impose punitive punishment. "I would've gotten jail time if Vic hadn't dropped the charges. The community service is purely punitive, 'cause the judge is tired of me. Jaclyn Love, you been in and out of here too much over the last ten years. I don't wanna see you again!"

With this setup, many writers would have made Kadan uptight, bougie, and judgmental and Jaclyn tragic. They might try to work the opposites-attract trope primarily based on class. Christina C. Jones does not do anything that simplistic. Jaclyn is going through some things, but she's also fabulous—beautiful, effervescent, spirited, and already beloved. Jac is also a small-business owner and a college student close to finishing her degree. They're not that different when you get past the surface. In fact, Jaclyn Love is exactly Dr. Kadan Davenport's type, and everyone knows it. When Jac brings a wounded stray cat into his veterinary clinic, his colleagues are amused because it's immediately obvious from the way Jac and Kadan greet each other that she's the woman who inflicted his black eye (and a knee to the groin). And yet, even as Kadan tries to act out indifference, he has to admit, at least to himself, that Jaclyn Love is his preferred type of crazy and fine:

> *So . . . I couldn't even front on Jaclyn. Ol' girl was fine. Like extra fine. Risk it all fine. Problem was, she was a lunatic, evidenced by her busting me in my shit in my own house, getting arrested on the street after—which I saw through the window after I looked out to make sure Jemma's assurance she'd left the building wasn't a lie— and now, her ass bringing an injured cat in a bowl of chicken in here.*
>
> *But Kadan, ain't that the type of shenanigans you're a sucker for? <- the question I could count on from anybody who knew me, especially if they laid eyes on Jaclyn. The locs, the deep brown skin, the lips, the thighs, goddamn. Her whole erratic thick snack situation was exactly my type. Like . . . exactly my type. Exactly.*

That repetition. The detail. Beyond being a sucker for drama, Kadan's thoughts reflect so many things, subtle and overt. Being inside his head, it's clear that this vet loves brown-skinned Black women, and he also appreciates Jac's bold, conscious style. To Kadan, "She looked like the afrocentric answer to everything that ailed me, especially as my eyes traveled lower, taking in the way she filled out the simple dress she was wearing." His instinctual attraction to Jac's brand of Black beauty permeates every interaction. The descriptions of her appearance are specific and loving:

> *There she was behind the counter, her locs tucked away underneath a vibrantly printed headwrap that popped against her deep brown*

skin. Big flat wooden disc earrings hung from her ears, swinging
as she turned to greet her customers—us. Her fuchsia-painted lips
curved into a big, pretty ass smile—maybe my first time seeing
that, and damn.

Given the politics of desirability and the sanctions Black
women often operate under, this kind of full-throated, heartfelt
celebration of beauty is not a small thing.

Jac's distinctive brand has multiple dimensions. In addition
to being beautiful and volatile, she's also more than a little pro-
fane. She and her sisters share jokes that are as explicit as they
are hilarious. Kadan loves her quick, irreverent personality. But
with her record and her brash attitude, she violates the standards
of femininity that are held up as ideal among Black folks with
upper-class aspirations. Jones doesn't hide the fact that this is
frowned on by some of Kadan's relatives, who represent the
town's Black establishment. The Black female judge who im-
poses Jaclyn's unusually harsh sentence is Kadan's aunt, and she
staunchly objects to Jac dating her nephew. But Kadan doesn't
play by her rules. And he's really clear about that, standing up
for Jac when Judge Cali Freeman tries to shame her.

Jones's depiction of Black class dynamics is very real. The
social dynamic around Jac and Kadan reflects the complexities
within Black families, especially socioeconomic diversity, which
is rarely reflected in mainstream (white-dominated) media.
Kadan's aunt looks down on Jaclyn, but Jac's cousin is one of
Kadan's best friends, and Jac is also related to some of the oldest
families in town. Families can belong to exclusive Black elite

institutions like the Links and Black sororities and have generational ties to Black institutions and still have members who are struggling economically and/or with the law. They can have elite ties and still not pass muster with aunts who practice the politics of respectability. That complexity was reflected in the BET (Black Entertainment Television) series *Being Mary Jane*, and it's brought to life in the Love Sisters series, but it's typically absent most everywhere else.

Black Spaces as Places of Safety and Solidarity

Though *Let Me Free You* and *I Think I Might Love You* are situated in contemporary American settings, they have so much in common with Cole's fictional African world of *How to Catch a Queen*. The protagonists all live and work in predominantly Black environments, work for themselves, and are reciprocally supported by Black community. In a still unequal and unjust world, one of the ways modern authors of romance bring a sense of justice and inclusion for marginalized characters within the literature of hope is to create pockets of freedom and empowerment, just spaces or refuges, within which their main characters can thrive.

Sometimes it's the tiny private space between two people against the world. At other times, it's bigger, a circle of friends who are like family, or extended families or small towns. In romances like K. J. Charles's queer historicals *A Seditious Affair* (The Society of Gentlemen series) and *Band Sinister* and Courtney Milan's feminist Victorian historical romance series The

Brothers Sinister, that safe space exists in the friendship circle or communal organization in which the usual rules of society don't apply and members hold each other's secrets dear. There is safety and power in numbers. Every romance carves out a version of the world that makes space for living happily ever after.

In *I Think I Might Love You*, just as in the Black romances of Alexandria House and Alyssa Cole, though, the world-building and Black infrastructure are comprehensive. These authors locate their stories in predominantly Black towns or towns with thriving Black communities within them, on Black university campuses, and in fictional Black nations. This is one of the ways they decenter whiteness. The Love Sisters operate in a connected universe with the Wright Brothers series and both are full of such settings. The same is true of House's McClain Brothers and Romey U series. Even though Black solidarity is largely communicated through setting, Jones clearly also conveys this racial consciousness in Jac's point of view. Like Issa Rae, Jaclyn Love is openly rooting for everybody Black. Even when she's doing something as simple and urgent as searching for a local vet, she's making a deliberate choice about who to support. As Jones writes, "A quick glance at their website showed enough melanin from the various images on the home screen that I was comfortable giving them my business."

Of Skinfolk, Kinfolk, and the HEA

If romance in general is the literature of hope, some Black romances can be seen as the literature of hope and progress, HEAs made possible by Black solidarity and community as well as love. And yet even in these books, it's clear that none of these Black communities are inherently safe spaces for all. Racism isn't front and center since these protagonists work hard to carve out lives that aren't dominated by its influence. But that doesn't mean their worlds are free from injustice or even free from white supremacy, which can be deeply internalized and take many forms. Along with their partners, these women work to build truly safe spaces for themselves and others within imperfect worlds. After Sage's immigration status is secured, she and Neil fend off attacks based on inherited hierarchies and expectations that should be extinct. The survival of Shanti's marriage hinges on equal partnership and the inclusion of women and marginalized groups in Njazan political life. Jaclyn literally fights people who denigrate her because of her size; the resulting criminal record places her outside of standards of Black respectability imposed by Black elites. In all three novels, the values and aspirations invoked in "I'm rooting for everybody Black" buck up against the received wisdom of "all skinfolk ain't kinfolk" without diminishing that quest for community and love. Some folks hold on to divisions that don't serve us, but we keep it moving and keep loving anyway. It's fascinating and affirming to see Black women triumph, supported by community on the way to their HEA.

Finding Queer Black Women in Romance. Finding Bits and Pieces of Me.

NICOLE M. JACKSON

E very time I sat down to write this essay, I kept thinking that I needed to do research. I thought I didn't know enough about queer Black women in romance, even as a queer Black woman in romance. I wouldn't say that I was necessarily wrong or right. There is so much about the history—or lack thereof—of representations of queer Black women in romance, on- and off-page, that has been purposely hidden or ignored and should be unpacked. And still, there are so many avenues one could look down to uncover just a piece of the iceberg that is queer Black women in romance, that maybe the story isn't about the research I or others need to do, but why I felt so unworthy to talk about it at all.

When planning my aborted research project, I decided to revisit some of my favorite Black lesbian romances in film and television. In my mind, the goal was to contextualize my lifelong search for queer Black women in the media I consumed. I wasted months creating a list that mostly made me smile, ruefully, just before I frowned. And in the end, I spent months putting off actually consuming that media, not because I disliked the films and television shows where I saw bits and pieces of me, but because I remembered the dull ache that too often came in the wake of that consumption. Somehow, I'd forgotten about that pain. With the distance of time and space, I'd created an image of *The Color Purple* (the film, not the book), *The Watermelon Woman*, and *Pariah*, for instance, that softened my memories of the viewing experiences. In my nostalgia, I enjoyed the movies unconditionally and if I cried, I convinced myself that all the tears I shed were full of happiness and affirmation, never terror or pain.

Through this process of avoidance and reflection, I came to realize something I had not before: that so much of what I eventually came to look for in romance books was shaped in reaction to what I'd found elsewhere. It wasn't the presence of queer Black women themselves—I had been blessed to see that in media and in my real life since forever—but images of them loving one another and loving themselves. Before I had the language to describe it, I was looking for queer Black women, like me, who got their HEAs, like I wanted; I wanted to see them in love and loved.

As a child I collected little scraps of information about queer Black elders, living and passed on. It wasn't a conscious decision, just a thing I did before I had the language to even ask myself why any of this trivia mattered. In high school, my first near-failing grade on an assignment (in a class that wasn't math) was when I practically plagiarized a very long biography of jazz singer Bessie Smith. Honestly, I hadn't meant to lift a sizable chunk of the book into my essay, but I'd been so enraptured by her story that I'd wanted my teacher to know—just in case he didn't—that she had been Black and dark skinned and fat and queer and amazing. Also, her music was fantastic. Still. I earned the C- he gave me, but I also appreciated the kind note he wrote at the end of my paper, telling me how happy he was that I'd found someone in history to look up to, but to learn how to paraphrase. I'm pretty sure I learned in the same class that my lord and savior Josephine Baker was queer and had seduced—or been seduced by?—Frida Kahlo.

I have vivid memories of seeing *The Color Purple* repeatedly throughout my adolescence. It was the kind of movie I watched with my family whenever it was on basic cable, and it was one of the first DVDs I owned. I remember focusing intently on that bar fight scene when Shug pulls a nosy Celie into her room. The sounds of the bar give way to the quiet. Celie, shyly, admits to Shug that Mister has never kissed her—not that she wants to be kissed by him. Shug kisses her instead. I always have to rewind that scene to watch it again, feeling some new emotion about it each time. It was certainly the first time I remember seeing two Black women and realizing that they were . . . different . . . and maybe they were different like me, or near enough like me that I could see myself on that screen.

I mean, like Celie, I'd also shared my first kiss with my female best friend in a naive and emotionally unfulfilled way.

Over the years, I'm certain that I relived this moment more times than I can remember. While watching *Pariah*, there was very little that I related to and yet I remember watching Alike lean against the glass on the bus taking her to college in California, where she hoped to start a new life. I felt the same, thinking surely that once I left California, I could become some version of myself that was fuller, broader, and more me. Hell, I even distinctly remember a season three episode of *Living Single*, when Maxine Shaw's former law school friend shows up and comes out as a lesbian. *Living Single* used to be one of my favorite shows, and as a child, I remember thinking that my adult life would look like the one I saw on the television. So to see a lesbian in the fabric of this show that seemed to hold so many of my hopes and dreams for the future gave me something more than representation. It gave me a window.

I give this short and disjointed autobiography mostly to explain why finding queer Black women in romance offered me something that other media did not and has not, something I had apparently been searching for all along. Over the years, I've searched for and found queer Black women on film and television and in music. So much music! But far too many of the stories I've found were unhappy, and not in the Bury Your Gays™ way, but in the Forever Alone kind of way. Or, in other words, so many of the stories about queer Black women that I've consumed over the years helped me see pieces of myself, but they did not inspire me to believe in the magic of a happily ever after.

I turned to romance looking for that, but once again, I did so unconsciously. I made a lot of TBR mistakes. I kissed . . . er, read a lot of ugly ducklings. Over time I had to ask myself hard and, at times, uncomfortable questions about what I was really looking for and why.

And of course, the best time to go on a soul-searching emotional journey was right in the middle of graduate school.

Getting through my doctorate program was difficult. I'd moved thousands of miles away from my family and the people who loved me. I struggled, as so many do, to make new friends and find a community where I felt like I fit. And on top of that, I went from a supportive intellectual environment to one full of nothing but potholes. Actually, *difficult* might actually be too kind, because I was hanging on by a thread. I was struggling to finish revising my master's thesis in history. In fact, I was weeks away from defending my thesis on American student activism in the 1970s and 1980s and I was tired. I was taking a full load of courses, serving as a teaching assistant, and trying to get a full draft of a document I often worried I wasn't smart enough to write. More nights than not, I fell asleep on my futon couch with books and newspaper articles littering the floor at my feet. Every day, I had to open that Word document to work on one more paragraph—just one more paragraph. I was well on the way to my first—but certainly not last—academic burnout when I decided to read some fan fiction instead of revising that same paragraph for the hundredth time.

Over the next few weeks, I put myself on a schedule, working a full day, writing for a few hours at night, and then reading all the fan fiction I could cram into the couple of hours before I fell asleep. By the time I passed my thesis defense, I had graduated to self-published romance and I remember that summer break mostly by the gay bars my friends and I went to downtown and the fiction I read. I was mostly reading m/f IR (male/female interracial) romance at first, but the beauty of indie and self-published romance was the seemingly limitless options. If I could articulate a desire and was willing to commit myself to a few hours of research, I usually found nearly exactly what I was looking for, and that freedom was wonderful, especially when school wasn't nearly as accommodating of my efforts.

So often in online bookish communities, people will pose a question that reads something like: "Why is there NO diverse romance?" "Where are all the QPOC in romance?" I always like the people who see those questions and assume the best of intentions and offer that anonymous user some recommendations. Sometimes I'm that person, but very often I am not, because when I stepped wholeheartedly into reading romance, I eventually wondered where the queer Black women were hiding. I could find heterosexual Black romance and IR romances with Black female protagonists and I could find gay and lesbian romances, but for a period of time I felt certain that these categories never met. As if there were no queer Black people.

As if I did not exist.

But then I found books by Rebekah Weatherspoon. And then Alyssa Cole. And then Brooklyn Wallace. And then Talia Hibbert. And then Chencia C. Higgins. And Fiona Zedde.

And I guess this is where I have been always heading on this strange autobiographical journey that began with avoidance and confusion, and memories of searching for my people as a natural occurrence, something dug deep in my bones. Every time I have looked for queer Black women, I have found them. And once I've found one, she's opened the door to another and then another and so on. But that initial urge to make lists and revisit, to recover what I had lost, was as much about my own faulty memory as the need to prove the existence of people and characters I already knew existed. I turned to romance to find queer Black women who were in love and loved, and I found them, and still, every so often, someone will ask where they all are, where are they hiding. Sometimes they will ask me where all the queer Black women in romance are hiding, as if I am not here, Black, queer, and writing and reading romance.

So, just in case someone is compelled to ask me—or other queer Black women—that question again, I wanted to walk briefly through my own history of finding queer Black people in romance.

Rebekah Weatherspoon was my gateway. I found her and WOCinRomance on Tumblr sometime around 2015. I'm a historian who is very shaky on dates, but I know it must have been 2015 because Tumblr was still the popping place to be online and it was right in between the time she'd published *Sated*, the final book in her Fit Trilogy, and the first of her Sugar Baby novellas, *So Sweet*. I read every book I could get my hands on, checking out e-books from a library back home and spending whatever I could spare from my meager stipend and student loans. Rebekah was witty and knowledgeable online and there were so many queer Black women in her backlist that I felt dizzy with the possibilities. Kayla, the female lead of the Sugar Baby novellas, is bi and surrounded by a friend group full of other QPOC. She's witty and no-nonsense, a little bit kinky and broke. How could I not relate? *At Her Feet* was a sexy and sad and thought-provoking revelation. Suzanne is kinky in a way I was not, broken in ways I understood, and eventually brave in a way I think we all wish we could be. And *Treasure* gave me butterflies. As I devoured Rebekah's backlist, I marveled at these four very different queer Black women she'd written. I love Rebekah's books, but I especially love that her books often allow me to see these slivers of myself, my Blackness, my nerdiness, and my queerness reflected back at me from new angles and in different ways. Her female main characters are inquisitive (sometimes nosy), smart-mouthed, some of them are fat, and they all yearn to be loved. When someone asks me, "Where are the queer Black women in romance?" Rebekah's name is the first on my list.

A good friend of mine recommended Alyssa Cole's *An Extraordinary Union*, the first book in the Loyal League series, with reservations. "I know you don't like historical romance and you might not like this one, but . . . ," she'd said to me. I had liked that book and its sequels, but *That Could Be Enough*, Cole's f/f (female/female) post–Revolutionary War novella, made me feel something more tender than like, something like love.

I don't have a coming-out story.

I'm bi.

I haven't always identified as such. When I shared that first kiss with my childhood friend, it was . . . normal? Didn't we all do that? And if not, why not? The dissolution of our lifelong friendship in middle school felt much more notable than that kiss or all the others that followed it. I casually dated boys in school and had crushes on girls, and in a city where most of my friends seemed to realize at some point or another that maybe they weren't really straight—or if they were, that was a realization they had to come to—labels have rarely been important to me. Like a lot of queer people, I've often felt the need to renegotiate my relationship with labels, but in my thirties, I've settled on identifying as bisexual and queer interchangeably. I prefer the latter for its broadness—even though I know that for others in my communities, it stings—but for me it works. I don't have a coming-out story. I never worried that my family would not love me because I was queer. I have not lost friends because of who I am. I'm lucky in some ways, yes, and when I read Alyssa Cole's *That Could Be Enough*, I saw yet another sliver of myself. Andromeda Stiel is an out lesbian in eighteenth-century New York trying to woo Mercy Alston, the repressed maid of Eliza Hamilton. While Mercy is terrified of love, Andromeda has come from nothing but love. Andromeda tells her lover, "Grandfather always told me that it didn't matter who a person loved, but how well they treated others and what they did to make this country and this world better," so eerily close to things my own grandfather had told me so many times throughout my life. While there are not nearly as many queer Black women in Cole's backlist just yet, I have felt so many of the same feelings of reflection as I have while reading Rebekah and watching *The Color Purple*.

I don't, however, want to overstate the presence of sapphic Black romances. There aren't nearly enough queer Black women in romance books and I don't think that can be overstated. The genre is years away from that being a hyperbolic statement. Somehow, in the midst of both diverse romances and queer romances moving into mainstream, traditionally published romance, there is a dearth of books that feature queer Black women. For lesbians or queer women in relationships with women, so much of what exists right now is centralized in very particular spaces: young adult books, small and independent sapphic imprints (including Fiona Zedde's entire body of work), and Alyssa Cole's body of work (*Once Ghosted, Twice Shy* and *How to Find a Princess*). There is sporadic representation of bi Black women, such as Talia Hibbert's *Take a Hint, Dani Brown*. The self-published options, however, are broader. There's Chencia C. Higgins's *Things Hoped For* and *Consolation Gifts*, Meka James's *Being Hospitable*, J. Nichole's *A Girl Like Me*, Christina C. Jones's *Something Like Love*, and G. L. Tomas's *Wander This World* and *The Love Bet*.

Still, this isn't enough.

Some of this lack is related to the general lacuna of sapphic romances, period. While mlm (men loving men) stories have flourished in fan fiction, self-published and indie romance, and recently in traditional romance publishing, the same has not been generally true for f/f and wlw stories. And the statistics are worse along various intersections of marginalization. This is why, even though I am often annoyed at people asking for diverse queer romances, I make these same recommendations anyway, even compiling them in a long Twitter thread in summer 2020 because organizing is how I process grief and confusion, and even happiness, I guess. And for the sake of organization, I would be remiss to ignore the history of queer Black women's representation in romance.

Ann Allen Shockley was a librarian, journalist, novelist, and literary critic. Shockley's romance novels *Loving Her* and *Say Jesus and Come to Me*, alongside her short story collection, *The Black and White of It*, center Black lesbians more often than not, and have so often been erased from the narrative of romance publishing. The erasure of Shockley's works is complicated. They do not read like modern genre romances; rather, they seem much more in conversation with the Black women's literature of the 1980s and 1990s of the likes of Alice Walker and Lorraine Hansberry. If the modern romance reader is focused on the HEA, Shockley's books are not. Instead, her books are realistic, uncomfortable, and unflinching in their confrontation of racism and homophobia in white and Black societies. And yet if you were looking for queer Black women in romance, until very recently, there were few options beyond the time capsule of Shockley's works, which were much more likely to be housed in academic libraries than in your local bookstore.

Still, Shockley's presence should make us all wonder about who else we have been missing. Who else have we erased from the romance conversation? Are there other romances with queer Black women that I have missed?

And I think this is where I've ended up on this journey. On the one hand, I have discovered that I'm oddly protective of queer Black women's stories. And on the other hand, there are not enough! So often the repetitive cycle of romance conversations on social media swing between two pendulums. On one side is the anger at the limitations of romance—more accurately, the limitations of mainstream, traditionally published romance— to make room for BIPOC authors and the LGBTQIA+ community, detailing the myriad ways they have been alternately shut out of access to traditional romance publishing or, once there, denied mainstream support. On the other side of the pendulum is the celebratory recounting of all the ways the past few years have been the site of a renaissance in diversity in romance. What I find funny and disheartening is how long it takes people to realize that so many of those BIPOC authors are also in the LGBTQIA+ community and that they—and their stories— have not been part of that renaissance.

And so I've arrived again at the rueful smiles—happiness for what I've found and sometimes more than uncertainty at what to make of the paltry numbers. And maybe this is why I felt so unworthy of telling this story; I wanted it to be optimistic. I wanted to be able to say that there have been dozens, even hundreds, of romance novels where I have seen my queer self, but I have not. I have done what people who look like me often do; I've found slivers of myself and constructed my own belonging in that mosaic, and I am better for it. But queer Black readers of romance should not have to piece themselves apart for the tiniest bit. They should be able to walk into a bookstore and be spoiled for choice. And the next time some tired student needs a release from her coursework, she should be able to find more options to build a queer Black girl TBR than she reasonably has time to read.

Although, if there's one thing I've learned about myself in recent years, it's that I have the capacity to be an optimist. I find comfort knowing that the authors who are writing about queer Black women now will be able to keep on doing so, and more of us will read their books and find those pieces of ourselves however we can.

Writing in the Gaps

Black Latinx in Romance

ADRIANA HERRERA

When I was asked to write this essay about Black Love, I first had to think about my own life, the places I lived, and how in each of those places those two words have been one and the same and in others it is a hard-fought space. I had to examine my own sense of my Blackness during my childhood and my adulthood. I had to think about what it is that feels different about being Black here in the States—where I've lived most of my adult life—to how it felt in the Dominican Republic, where I was born and lived until I was twenty-three. What it was like to live in Eastern Africa, where the deep roots of culture and history are so vast and far-reaching. How that experience changed me. How the meaning of Blackness expanded and deepened when I lived in Africa and was engulfed in a seamlessly endless universe of Black people, languages, land, nations.

When I think of Black Love I think of the diaspora. Of the

diaspora that exists because of the slave trade. And the diaspora of Afro-Dominicans who, like me, have left home and built lives all over the world. Black Love, like Blackness, is something intrinsically tied to our own particular lived experience, but rooted in a larger history, in a larger communal experience. Black Love is powerfully enduring. I don't know if there is an institution that has been tested more than the Black family, and yet it remains unbroken. Black Love made me, literally, and it formed me figuratively. And yet, my awareness of just how hard-fought that love was didn't arrive in my consciousness until my adulthood.

I grew up in the Dominican Republic. I was born in the capital, Santo Domingo. Afro-Dominican identity can be as slippery as it is firmly grounded in my homeland. Despite being inexorably linked to Haiti (which abolished slavery on the entire island in 1801), the very first Black republic, our soil being the literal birthplace of Black Liberation, the narrative of our racial identity is . . . problematic. Being born and raised on an island that's predominantly Black, but where the white elites have systematically proffered a narrative of Eurocentric ancestry can be . . . a mindfuck. Culturally and historically, interracial relationships have been the norm in the Dominican Republic, and overwhelmingly, Dominicans are Afro-descendant. And yet our Blackness is not named or examined as central to us.

My father and mother are both Black, and yet it was never something that was a distinction, something that was seen to have a bearing on our lived experience. We were all Dominican first, and that was the defining characteristic. It was in the DR that I began reading romance when I was still in elementary school. I started with translated young adult romances that my mother would buy for me. These were not Dominican books; they were Spanish translations of a series about an Austrian princess. I imagine that somewhere in my mind it must have registered that the physical descriptions of the people in the books had nothing to do with me. They certainly were not about Black Love, but I must have just accepted that even if in my real life, Black Love was all around me, I was not going to get it in the pages of the books I read. And that was about the books, in part, but it was also about the lack of nuance in Dominican culture regarding race. Regarding our real roots. Blackness was everywhere, but unspoken. Our African roots clearly visible but unexamined and unrecognized. And I wonder if that was how I read romance then . . . not clearly aware that I was missing in those pages.

There is a well-known Dominican actress, Chiqui Vicioso, who likes to say that she didn't know she was Black until she immigrated to the United States. That's something I've said about my own experience many times, too. I learned to be more curious about my Afro-descendance here in the States. My own sense of my race was something that remained only superficially explored until I was confronted with a different reality here. And it probably would still be an abstract thing if, in 2002, at the age of twenty-three, I hadn't left my homeland and come to New York City. Moving to New York meant that I had to reexamine my identity. That I had to grapple with being seen differently. In the DR we are all Dominican first, and it's implied that we are mostly brown (of all shades). But here, I was not just Dominican. I was Black, I was Latina—I was a foreigner. I was Black on sight, then Latina when I opened my mouth and spoke Spanish . . . then at the very end, I was Dominican. And those things didn't seem to be able to blend together as seamlessly as they did back home. I felt compelled to pick a side. Was I Latina, was I Black? I decided I was both . . . and that was its own challenge. I found that asserting my Blackness and all that it entailed within Latinx communities could be contentious, and claiming a place as a Black woman was complicated.

My connection to and awareness of my Blackness was awakened in New York. I'd read Audre Lorde and James Baldwin in college, but their writing felt very different as I read it here in the States. I understood how isolating and disconnected Blackness could feel when you are in the minority, and how important it was to understand the legacy of my roots and examine my place in the diaspora. My move to New York also meant my break with romance. As my own connection to my Blackness evolved, my awareness of how people like me were treated (or erased) in fiction increased. This, paired with my commitment to feminist values, made it hard to find refuge in the genre that for so long had been a comfort for me.

Three years after arriving in New York City, I got married and moved to Addis Ababa, Ethiopia, and that was a discovery. In Addis I could be in a way I had not been able to be anywhere else. Blackness and the many colors, shapes, sounds of it was a given. I could be a Black woman who spoke Spanish, unquestionably. The depth and width of Blackness was not an idea or a faraway notion. It was a mere fact that Black people could be from different places, speak different languages, be blended in a million different ways and still be firmly rooted in Africa. Black Love in Ethiopia didn't need a qualifier, it's the same as Ethiopian Love. And it was in Ethiopia that I came back to romance. Not on my first time living there, but later in my early thirties when I desperately needed a safe haven, when my own life was in turmoil.

After Ethiopia, I lived in Honduras. There, I worked with the Garifuna people, Afro-descendant Hondurans who live on the coastal areas of Honduras and Nicaragua. In those communities, I was a "prima," a distant cousin from the same family tree. Among the Garifuna people, I could hear and see myself clearly. Their tastes and sounds so intimately linked to the ones of my own homeland, and yet distinct and uniquely theirs. Honduras was another place that cemented and deepened for me the notion of Blackness as a vast universe. For the Garifunas who escaped genocide and found ways to preserve their language and culture in the face of brutal discrimination, Black Love is Garifuna Love. And that brings me to Black Love here in the States, the place that I've called home for most of my adult life. Here, those two words feel a lot harder won.

As I consider my journey as a romance reader and later a romance writer, I can't help but see a parallel in how I've consumed books and my own journey in understanding myself. The way I've engaged with love stories in fiction mirrors how my own consciousness has changed and evolved. Today, I proudly write romance, and for many years now have openly talked about my passion for genre fiction, but that was not always the case. I've had to grow into that. I had to shift my own sense of myself as a lover of romance before I could claim my place in that community. I've had to look back and recognize the places where my love of romance awakened and saved me. Which means I have to go back to the beginning: my love for telenovelas.

Telenovelas are the quintessential form of Latinx entertainment. Life revolved around those torrid stories of love during my childhood. Unfortunately, as much as they were a central part of Latinx culture, Black Latinx were never really part of the picture. Black Latinx roots go back five hundred years, and yet when you consider who is represented as Latinx in media or in fiction, ours are not the faces you see.

There are many kinds of telenovelas: working-class dramas, teen telenovelas, and even historical. Latinx people love their over-the-top love romance. But if you watched every one of the most popular telenovelas of all time, you'd have a hard time finding a Black person in them. According to IMDB's database, since the late 1950s, more than eight hundred telenovelas have been produced and broadcast. Among the ones the database selected as the Top 100 telenovelas of all time, not a single one of them had a Black Latinx protagonist.

Imagine me as a nine-year-old girl in Santo Domingo in 1987 and settling in to watch *Quinceañera*. It's the first telenovela I remember following from beginning to end. And the one that launched Thalia as a superstar. In *Quinceañera*, Thalia is a wealthy, innocent girl who falls for a working-class mechanic, and their romance revolves around the hurdles they have to over-come. I was entranced by the forbidden love between the pro-tagonists. But as much as I adored the drama and the romance, other than speaking Spanish, the Mexican actors on the screen didn't look or live like me. Other than the fact that they were also Latin, I had as much in common with those characters as I had with any of the people in American sitcoms I watched on cable. Then finally when I was eighteen, *Xica da Silva*, a Brazil-ian telenovela, was announced—and the heroine was a gorgeous Afro-Latina. Finally, a woman, a heroine, who looked like me in a telenovela. The excitement was short-lived.

Xica da Silva was the story of a slave girl who "captivates" the white hero so completely, he asks that she be given to him as a gift. His great demonstration of love was granting her freedom and installing her as his official concubine. I remember the night *Xica da Silva* premiered in the DR. They'd been teasing a clip with Xica's naked back. It was scandalous and the entire country was buzzing. Everyone was speculating on whether they'd actu-ally show her fully nude or cut to commercial. I honestly can't remember if they showed her or not. What I do remember is the tone in conversations about Xica and the actress who played her.

Xica da Silva was the first moment I gained a solid notion of the impact representation can have. Because after watching liter-ally hundreds of telenovelas—which admittedly were rife with problematic themes from misogyny to classism and everything in between—what finally made me give up on them was the first one that had a protagonist who looked like me. I was so disap-pointed. I remember thinking even then that I'd never seen a telenovela heroine objectified in that way. Xica was wicked and vindictive, a woman who used her sexuality as a weapon. Whose carnality was so overt, the hero had to own her the moment he saw her. Which, considering that Taís Araújo, the actress who played Xica, was only seventeen when they filmed the show, makes the whole thing even more sordid.

I clearly saw the difference in how the lighter-skinned or white heroines in other telenovelas were portrayed. There was an assumption of purity and lack of sexual knowledge in them that enraptured the heroes. That innocence presumably made them worth the wait and all the sacrifice winning their love entailed. Heroines like Thalia in *Quinceañera* were untouched and untainted. Xica was a temptress. As I began to see myself differently, as I began to explore feminism and my own sexuality, telenovelas lost me. But I still had romance.

Historical romance was what I gravitated to and really where I cemented my love of the genre; by my late teens I was a devoted reader of the genre. There, too, I had to learn to find glimpses of myself, grit my teeth through POC being depicted as virtual caricatures, and overlook the way the place I was from was constantly talked about in throwaway phrases. In one page I'd get a detailed, fanciful description of the British Isles, learn about the many distinctions in the accents from region to region, and in the next I'd see a mention of a character escaping to the "West Indies" or seeking fortune in the "colonies," and imagine that somewhere in those three words, I could see part of my ancestry.

The West Indies are thousands of islands, dozens of languages. My homeland has been described as "the cradle of blackness in the Americas." The labor (and exploitation) of the people in those little islands in the Caribbean Sea built the palaces and manors where these heroes and heroines traipsed around, sipping brandy. As much as I loved the romances, it frayed (it still does) how inconsequential we were in romance. That's why eventually I had to leave historical romance, too. As I leaned in to understanding more about Black feminism, misogyny, and agency, I couldn't reconcile those values and the history I was beginning to understand with some of the more problematic parts of the genre I loved.

I found romance again in my early thirties after my father died. In Ethiopia, I had a wonderful and emotionally draining job; I was a young mother and I was grieving my father. I felt untethered and crushed. On a whim I downloaded a couple of romances into my e-reader, and a few weeks later, I'd read a dozen more, and for the first time in months, I felt comforted. I found queer romance; from Josh Lanyon to Radclyffe, I devoured them all. I could not get enough of stories about gay men and women finding love that didn't end in tragedy. That discovery was the watershed that brought me fully back into the genre. I returned to romance after a long absence and discovered that, like me, the genre had changed . . . for the better. I was different and the stories were different, too, nowhere near perfect or even inclusive, but there was romance I could read and enjoy. There were feminist, kickass heroines I could root for. There was explicit consent on the page, and it made me hopeful I would soon be able to see my whole self in some of the romance I was reading. Romance got me through grieving my father, and it made perfect sense. After all, it was my parents who taught me to love romance.

For decades my father was known as the Dominican "Rey de las Telenovelas." He got into the business of television as a young man, and in 1968 when he was thirty years old, he brought *Renzo el Gitano*, a Mexican telenovela, to Dominican viewers. It was the first time a televised drama was broadcast in the DR, and it was a national sensation. It made him a wealthy man in the span of a few months and put him on the path to a very long and successful career. For decades he purchased the broadcasting rights for dozens, possibly hundreds of telenovelas. My mother worked with him, selling commercial airtime to advertisers. From both my father and my mother I learned to never underestimate the appeal of a good love story. My father taught me that a good romance made for a very sound investment. One year I remember my father bought himself a sky-blue, brand-new Mercedes-Benz he jokingly nicknamed after the telenovela that had filled the coffers that season. My parents not only understood how irresistible a good romance can be, they banked on it.

Some of my only memories of my parents together are of them in business conversations, in which they talked about the performances of the telenovelas currently airing or the potential of those in production. They'd vigorously speculate which ones would be a hit. To this day my mother has an almost encyclopedic knowledge of which telenovelas were hits in the '70s, '80s, and '90s. She can tell me which actors had the biggest success and even which tropes were popular over the decades. One day

I asked her how she still remembered all of it and she said, "I remember the paychecks!"

On paper my mother and father's love story had the makings of a great romance. They met when my father was already a successful businessman, and my mother was a stunning caramel-skinned college student and part-time fashion model, twenty years his junior. In the books I write—and love to read—their story would be the stuff of an epic HEA. Real life didn't quite turn out that way. As well as my parents worked together in business—and their keen understanding of what entailed a good HEA yielded them great financial success—that insight didn't quite translate to their own relationship.

I think a lot about that dichotomy, and I can't help but wonder what it would have been like for my father to have seen men who looked like him be heroes of the stories he bought and sold. If he could've seen actors with his wiry hair, wide strong nose, and deep brown skin as the heartthrobs of a story. What it would've been for my mother to see a woman like her with silk-pressed hair and caramel skin be the one who was worth sacrificing everything for. I wonder if that would've helped them believe in their own story a little more.

I'm now the second generation in my Afro-Dominican family who sells love stories. I love that legacy and I strive to honor it. The difference of course is that my parents sold love stories about people who shared their language, but not much else. The actors on the screen didn't have much in common with my parents' lived experience in any real or significant way, and I make it my mission to write love stories that center and represent all my intersecting identities. Even though they could not sell love stories like theirs, the path they blazed, the example they gave me, granted me the boldness and ability to dream bigger. I don't think I would write the books I do if I hadn't seen my parents achieve what they did.

But even so, I was a Dominican woman, and as far as I knew (and the shelves in bookstores confirmed this), we didn't write romance novels. So even when I had stories in me, I let myself be content with reading other people's stories, until I couldn't do that anymore. What pushed me to start writing romance was a moment of transformed consciousness. In *Black Feminist Thought*, Patricia Hill Collins talks about "a connection between experience and consciousness that shapes the individual everyday lives of [Black] women." I think about that constantly, and it was this exact experience that finally gave me the impetus to start writing.

On my return to the US after almost ten years abroad, I shifted my work from international NGO to advocacy work with marginalized communities here in the States. Through my clients and the work I was doing, I constantly came up against gatekeepers and bureaucracies that were not built for the people I served. People who lived at the intersection of multiple marginalized identities and simply were not seen by the system. It was frustrating and gratifying all at once, and it opened my eyes once again to many more things I had not known. And then 2016 happened and everything changed again. Like so many others, I was scared. The conversation around immigrants in this country was terrifying and I was actively fearful for my clients, many of whom were undocumented. I turned to romance for comfort, as I've done so many times in my life, and it felt like it was betraying me, too. There was not much that reflected my experience or the experiences of the people I worked with. As a reader, I felt impatient and restless, as more time passed and little changed when it came to representation in the genre. Still, it didn't occur to me that I could step into the arena and make space with my own stories.

For a while, I'd been toying with the idea of writing a queer romance about a group of Afro-Caribbean friends who grew up together in the Bronx. It was just a thought that had been on the back burner of my brain and that I kept going back to for months, but then I was called to action. I was in the audience of a panel about feminism in romance and heard one of the most successful voices in the genre dismiss out of hand the idea that marginalized people could exist in her books. She explained that the likelihood of a marginalized character getting a happy ending was so farfetched the story would have to be about proving POC could exist happily, and the romance would be lost. It broke my heart to realize that one of the most lauded voices in the genre could not imagine my ancestors getting a happy ending or that it was even a possibility they could've been seen as a part of society at all. That was the moment when it became clear to me that if I wanted to see Afro-Caribbean stories in romance with the nuance and depth I believed we deserved, I needed to write them.

I came into romance with a mission, to write stories about people who look like my people getting unapologetic happy endings. My people are Latinx, yes, but Latinx is not a race; Black is my race and that of the people I write in my books. To write Black Latinx Love *is* to write Black Love. We assert that Black people are not a monolith, but then we also must intentionally create space for that to blossom and grow. Part of what we do by claiming space for our singular story is to do away with the idea that we are interchangeable. That my story about a Dominican queer woman somehow should speak for every other Spanish-speaking Latinx, or that because my Black characters identify themselves as Black and they speak Spanish, their stories don't fit in some Black spaces.

I write about people who look and sound like my people. My people are from a little island in the Caribbean to whose shores the transatlantic slave trade first arrived. Santo Domingo, the city I was born and raised in, where I went to kindergarten and college, has been described as "the cradle of blackness in the Americas." The first documented mention of Africans in the Americas goes back to 1501, when Nicolás de Ovando requested the Spanish Crown's permission to bring slaves to Hispaniola. By 1519 the indigenous population had virtually vanished, and African slaves were brought to replace them in the mines and wherever the labor of exploiting our land had to be done. In 1520, there were twenty thousand African slaves in Hispaniola (and within the next few decades their presence would grow to be nine out of ten people on the island). The first slave rebellion recorded was in 1522.

Caribbean roots have many branches, some deeper than others, but the ones that bind us together are those of the African ancestors that we share. Our colonizers' languages divide us and our African ancestry unites us. According to the PBS documentary *Black in Latin America*, "the real black experience, in terms of numbers, is all throughout the Caribbean and Latin America." Out of the more than 11 million men and women brought to the Americas as slaves, about 10 million of them went to the Caribbean and South America—almost 40 percent just to Brazil. I don't write Black adjacent stories because my characters are Latinx, I write Black stories because my Afro-descendant Latinx characters are part of the diaspora. If they sound different and come from different places, that just cements the fact that our world is wide and magnificently diverse, and we deserve to see all of it in our stories.

I hope my stories help turn those little gaps where I had to imagine myself as a kid into wide-open spaces. To blow out the little crevices where we've been allowed to exist, and make room for everyone who wants to tell their own particular story. That's why in the Dreamers series I had the GA Crew: a group of friends whose families came from Cuba, Jamaica, Haiti, the Dominican Republic, and Puerto Rico, the biggest islands in the Caribbean. I wanted to not only show the ties that bind us together (even if we had different colonizers) but also the complexity of our culture. That's why now, as I delve more into the historical space, I am trying to build a container for those stories where Afro-Latinx people are the center. It is time that the word *Latinx* stops representing only one kind of experience and is understood for the colossal container that it is. A space full of stories of resilience and of love that triumph; so much of that love happens to be Black.

How a Black Author Found Her Romance History

MARGO HENDRICKS

S he grew up in a home where books and reading are highly valued and a library card proved an invaluable gift to a young Black girl learning to read. Her imagination soared untethered by the everyday tugs of life. She came to love the worlds she found between book covers and gave faces and vocal tones to the people inside. She entered buildings and followed roads into deserts and rivers, mountains, and cities far removed from her small California city. Lost in a book, she sometimes forgot to do her chores or didn't hear her grandmother's stern voice. School nights were the worst, and the flashlight beneath the bed covers often betrayed her. Yet she couldn't leave the magic of words, of images, and of distant places she hoped one day to visit: Egypt. Mali. England. Ireland. China. Palestine. Ghana. Her library card became her most prized possession. Little did this young Black reader imagine that one day she would write the words "I am a Black academic, romance reading author" as a way of introduction.

Teaching Romance

When first sharing my love of the romance genre within academic circles, a number of my peers assumed I referred to pre/early modern texts such as *The Faerie Queene* or *Orlando Furioso* or *Gerusalemme liberata*—romances written pre-1700s and in forms that have since become obsolete within the genre. When I told my peers the romances were contemporary romance novels, i.e., genre fiction, a noticeable shift in their demeanor occurred. Most often it was a physical sign, a slightly raised forehead or a faint look of dismissal. On the rare engagement that led to questions, the person would ask why I read "genre fiction," and to their mind not very good genre fiction at that. Such attitudes have plagued the romance genre from its inception, yet the romance has remained the most popular and profitable of literary genres. What these peers refused to acknowledge is that literature is neither static nor inflexible. The texts mentioned at the beginning of this essay are early forms of romance and largely read within an academic arena, and rarely by readers not involved in the study of pre-seventeenth-century European cultures or literatures.

I am an academic, a Black professor who writes and researches on race, gender, and early modern English culture. Without question, I chose my area of study based on my childhood readings. I have always been fascinated by history and its depiction in fiction. I have always been a fiction reader, and growing up, it didn't matter what genre—historical fiction, science or speculative fiction, fantasy, or the so-called "classics." If there were words on the page, it was my jam. I also wrote scripts based on what I read, involving cousins in reenactments of scenes from some favorite childhood books—Frank Yerby's *The Saracen Blade*, Margaret Irwin's *Elizabeth, Captive Princess*, Margaret Campbell Barnes's *The Passionate Brood*, or W. E. B. Du Bois's *Dark Princess: A Romance*. As a precocious reader (these books were read between ages ten and thirteen), I assumed all these writers with the exception of Du Bois were white. It wasn't until high school that I learned Frank Yerby, a bestselling author of white-centric historical fiction, was also an African American novelist. Along with Irwin and Barnes, Yerby's non-US historical fiction shaped my interest in medieval and Renaissance European history and chivalric literature.

Yerby's *The Saracen Blade* tells the story of a thirteenth-century serf, Pietro di Donati, born the same moment as Emperor Frederick II. Donati's chivalric quest for knightly glory and the love of an aristocratic woman is against the political, religious, and military background of the Christian fight to reclaim the "Holy Land" from Islamic sovereignty. Du Bois's *Dark Princess*, while set in the twentieth century, similarly engages chivalric ideology and tropes. Instead of a thirteenth-century Italian serf as a heroic figure, Du Bois gave his readers Matthew Townes, a self-exiled Black medical student living in Berlin. Similar to Donati, Townes is drawn into a chivalric quest not just for identity and belonging but for the love of a woman whose class and privilege normally puts her beyond his reach. The

South Asian Indian princess draws him into a world of revolutionary politics and intellectual and artistic life. Ultimately, after a life in US (Chicago) politics, including a political marriage, Townes reunites with Princess Kautilya and fathers her child, who becomes a maharaja.

In different ways, Yerby's historical fiction and Du Bois's romance novel helped to define my reading habits, and eventually my academic career. These novels influenced my engagement with chivalric or quest romance. More specifically, Du Bois's dedication in *Dark Princess* sent me scurrying to Edmund Spenser's epic romance *The Faerie Queene*. As a college and university faculty member, I taught several romance literature classes. The first one was while I was at an urban state college in California. The syllabus was 80 percent late-twentieth-century authors and 90 percent historical romance novels. The one Black-authored novel on the list was Octavia Butler's *Wild Seed*, and of course, there was some pushback because students viewed the book not as romance but solely as science or speculative fiction. The novel begins in seventeenth-century Africa and moves to the English settler colonies in the Americas. Doro is a "breeder" of unique people (telepaths, telekinetics, and empaths). When his "seed" villages in Western Africa are destroyed, he senses the presence of an unusual supernatural, Anyanwu—a shape-changer. Butler's novel details the complex love/hate relationship between these two powerful figures as it plays out against a settler colonialist history embodied in the enslavement of Black bodies. What these mostly white students resisted were two features of the book. First, the paranormal elements of shape-shifting and cannibalistic vampirism in *Wild Seed* appeared outside the normative conventions of traditional late-twentieth-century historical romances. The novel did not deal with an aristocratic class or offer a conventional happily ever after. In fact, many of my students questioned whether we should view Butler's novel as even a love story. What they didn't question was the historical setting or the complex relationship between African natives Anyanwu and Doro. In the end, I acknowledge the students' arguments that it was a stretch to label *Wild Seed* a romance novel, but the beauty was in the exploration.

Even while reading *Wild Seed*, a number of students resisted seeing the novel as a romance. While the ending was not a conventionally depicted happily ever after, the paranormal elements did not mean there wasn't one—it was an HEA that worked within the dynamics of the relationship between Anyanwu and Doro. For these students who expected a "profess your love, get married, and have children" ending, Butler's world-building overshadowed the way students read the novel's romance. The unspoken narrative in the class, and a perception or response familiar to Black romance authors and readers, was the question of relatability. Students, many who considered themselves liberals or progressives, resisted seeing the relationship between Doro and Anyanwu in terms of romance conventions, especially since most viewed Doro as the antagonist, and the relationship between the main characters was always one of power and thus negated the possibility of a potential happily ever after. Yet, as I pushed the class past this marker, what I also unearthed was a perspective that surfaces frequently in discussions of Black romance and Black love: a belief that Black people, especially enslaved Black peoples, were either incapable of love or experienced a different kind of love than what (to the students' minds) is represented in traditional romance narratives. In essence, agency over their emotions was not seen as part of Black subjectivity.

A year after teaching this course, I moved to a predominantly white research university where the majority of my teaching took place in my academic "field" (Renaissance and early modern English literature). These courses were framed by critical race theory, Black feminist theory, and intersectionality. Resistance to these critical and theoretical lenses came largely from white male students. The challenges were most acute when I critiqued Eurocentric notions of love, beauty standards and appearance, sexuality, and class. In a course on race and early modern English romance, I taught sections of several texts, including the English translations of Ludovico Ariosto's *Orlando Furioso* and Torquato Tasso's *Gerusalemme liberata* (translated into English as *Jerusalem Delivered*) and Edmund Spenser's *The Faerie Queene*. Each of these texts depicted African-born or descended characters, and in most cases the African-descended women were royalty or nobility. The other commonality among these works was the world-building. Each of these texts dealt with the medieval conflict between Muslims and Christians. It was in this class that I encouraged an exploration of the relationship between white supremacist ideologies about who deserves love and who does not, especially in the romance epic poem *Jerusalem Delivered*.

The source for *Jerusalem Delivered* was the third-century Greek romance novel the *Aethiopica*. The story line for both romances is the Black monarchs of Ethiopia have a white daughter. The daughter is secretly carried away and eventually becomes the adoptive child of a wealthy Greek. The heroine, Charikleia, meets and falls in love with the hero, Theagenes. After a series of adventures, Charikleia is reunited with her biological parents, who accept Theagenes, and the couple achieve their happily ever after. *Jerusalem Delivered* tweaks the ending. The heroine (Clorinda) and hero (Tancred) die days after Clorinda discovers she is "white passing" since her biological parents are Black and the monarchs of Ethiopia. The discussion points I posed to the class ranged from why her "Ethiopian" interiority is a problem to why it was necessary for Tasso (and his English translator) to deny Clorinda and Tancred the romance ending that readers would expect, having read *Jerusalem Delivered*'s source text.

It didn't surprise me when most of the students ignored the matter of Charikleia and Clorinda's "Ethiopian" lineage. Instead, the students appeared more comfortable theorizing about tragic narrative fault lines or, in several instances, the ideological significance of the conflict between Christianity and Islam in *Jerusalem Delivered* than engaging the issue of the "white Ethiopian." Even more telling was a nervousness about the idea of seeing the heroines as "white passing" subjects. What didn't surprise me in the end was the one essay that figured Clorinda as a "tragic mulatta" (completely ignoring Charikleia), read her as a romance precursor to Nella Larsen's "white passing" Clare Kendry, and suggestively concluded Black people rarely experience happily ever afters. I walked away from that pedagogical moment with a more nuanced understanding of the complex ways white supremacy's ideologies inform cultural expectations about a literary genre like romance. What I might ask the students now: Why is it hard to resist the idea of the tragic white passing subject? Why is it necessary to "relate" to the representations of specifically Black love? And what do unconscious racist logic and literary elitism have to do with the way they read romance in general, and non-white romance fiction in particular? What I also realized, although I have been long aware of this point, is that an insistence on objectivity is not a default position when it comes to reading Black romance or romance where the protagonist(s) are Black.

In hindsight, the question that I failed to ask the students, and what I would pose to readers new to Black romance (or any non-white romance fiction) who insist on "relatability," is what does that entail? What specifically would make the characters "relatable" to you? Is it your lived experience or the expectation that fictional characters must reflect that experience underscoring your reading? What racializing expectations do you bring with you as a reader? And, most important, can you engage in anti-racist reading? It is these questions, in my opinion, that most romance readers need to ask themselves before they read any romance, and especially romances that center Black characters and Black happily ever afters.

Reading Black Historical Romance

When I graduated from high school in 1966, I chose not to pursue college and went straight to work. I had cut my "romance eyeteeth" on white-authored historical fiction as a ten- and eleven-year-old, which I suspect made it easy to graduate to white-authored historical romance fiction in my twenties. None of these romances featured main characters other than white women and men. Even Bertrice Small's *The Kadin* (1978) was little more than an exotic "harem romance." Her Scotland-born heroine, despite being the "mother" of Suleiman and, as she claims, having given most of her adult life to the Ottoman Empire, returns to Scotland, concealing her "other life," and oversees her family's social status. Of course, she dies happily in her native land. For the most part, my historical romance reading centered on story lines focused on England, even if the author (as Small did) added a non-English location for exoticism. Not until I read Kathleen Woodiwiss's *The Flame and the Flower* (1972) did I read a romance that simultaneously entertained and worked a nerve. The setting was antebellum Virginia and the hero an aristocratic-born enslaver. It was this historical romance (and two subsequent Woodiwiss books) that nearly ended my relationship with the historical romance subgenre. As someone politicized during the seventies and eighties, I found it difficult to reconcile the problematic and stereotypical depictions of non-white peoples and/or the idealization of societies that rendered the exploitation of non-white peoples invisible. I also wanted to read story lines that increasingly reflected the love and relationships Black couples had despite societal constraints.

I didn't stop reading historical romances, though, and voraciously consumed the books of Johanna Lindsey, Rosemary Rogers, Jennifer Wilde, and Laurie McBain, among others.

Reading these novels, I set aside my lived experiences. I grew up in a segregated community of primarily Black and Mexican peoples, along with a tiny population of Japanese and Korean peoples, and despite the racism, I witnessed love stories playing out around me. What I didn't see in the historical romances I read were those stories. I eventually turned away from romance to read speculative fiction and fantasy. I returned to historical romances when a coworker recommended Beverly Jenkins's *Night Song*. Set in 1882 Kansas, *Night Song* tells the story of schoolteacher Cara Lee Henson and Sergeant Chase Jefferson of the Tenth Calvary, whose love emerges in the aftermath of the US Civil War and in the midst of Jim Crow laws. Despite Chase's determined advances, Cara is equally determined to protect her reputation and teaching position. Yet neither can deny the powerful spark ignited by a chance meeting two years later. As Cara and Chase's passionate romance develops, it is soon threatened by the moralistic dictates of a wealthy and powerful woman, Virginia Sutton, and her vindictive son Miles's obsession with Cara. Where Miles fails, Chase succeeds and wins Cara's heart.

Night Song was the first historical romance where, as a Black romance reader, I felt respected, loved, and seen. To lose myself in a wonderfully researched romance about two individuals whose lives and love are affected by the racism of nineteenth-century United States but not destroyed by it was a genuine pleasure. More important, to read a romance not weighted by European standards of beauty but which actually celebrates the variety of Black women's beauty. I have since read every historical romance Jenkins has written, and added to my list the works of authors like Alyssa Cole, Vanessa Riley, Piper Huguley, Rebel Carter, and Chanta Rand. The love stories created by these writers, some based on historical figures and others wholly fictional, offer the complexities of Black lives, Black love, and Black communities through history.

For all readers, I would argue, a decision to read a romance novel instead of another type of literature is multilayered. In addition to a love story and a satisfying resolution, readers are also drawn to well-developed characters that are familiar and recognizable, world-building that is believable, and a compelling narrative. Readers bring to the romance novel not just a set of expectations about the genre, however. Romance readers also bring with them explicit and implicit notions of race and romance. In part, these notions are based on the reader's socioeconomic position. In a more fundamental way, these expectations are often manifestations of the prevailing ideologies about the naturalness of white-centered romance narratives. For example, white main characters are rarely defined in terms of their skin color, and thus are racially unmarked, while depictions of nonwhite characters are described based on color or ethnicity. For white readers of romance, not understanding the privileges afforded by white supremacy, to not see "whiteness," often creates a blind spot among those same readers when it comes to representations of Black characters and Black love.

To illustrate this point, I want to draw attention to a recent interracial romance novel, Naima Simone's *Back in the Texan's Bed*. The scene is when the main characters, Charlotte and Ross, meet again after three years: "Pain, because for the first time in three years she stared into the beautiful cold face of the man she'd once loved" (18). We are told that Charlotte, a chef, is a Black woman almost from the start; the "restaurant was managed by a black woman. The kitchen was run by a black woman" (16). Yet the reader's only physical reference to Ross's presumed race or color is when he and Charlotte come face-to-face in the restaurant and she "couldn't jerk her gaze away from a pair of icy blue eyes" (18). The only reference to Ross's color occurs in the description of "his golden skin [which] remained as unblemished and smooth as ever" (33). While on the surface such descriptions may seem insignificant, what they allude to is the powerful effect white supremacy has on our reading. Whiteness as a racializing marker goes unnamed in most romances, including ones where one of the characters is non-white. Our only clues are found in the contrasts: Black woman versus a man with "icy blue eyes" and "golden skin," presumably a reference to a tan.

Other factors, such as wealth and class, also work to redirect the reader's "gaze" toward unproblematic whiteness. Inequality between love interests is often couched in terms of white wealth versus Black or other non-white working or middle class rise to success. *Night Song* depicts the economic, historical, and political inequalities that led to the creation of the town of Henry Adams and other Black towns like it, as well as how Black people mitigated the impact of those inequalities. In other words, as a Black romance set entirely in a Black community, *Night Song* makes the default Blackness rather than whiteness, and that default is visible. The novel also refuses to sanction white expectations about Black people and what white romance readers might find relatable: the idolization of Black trauma or suffering, extreme poverty, or the abjection of enslavement. Finally, while not explicitly stated, Jenkins's historical romances are not written for a white gaze and, not surprisingly, this is a factor—one shared by many Black authors writing romance fiction—that often troubles white romance readers. These readers have been "trained" to unsee whiteness in romance, to view whiteness as a default, and, when that default is challenged or made obvious, to call into question the historical authenticity or representational accuracy of story lines, class representations, and physical appearances where whiteness is not the norm.

Teaching and reading romance have led me to wonder why Black and non-white readers of romance do not suffer similar blind spots. The answer to this question warrants a more rigorous analysis than I can offer here; however, I believe the key is centered in the cultural silence around the role of whiteness as the de facto given of the historical romance narrative. While suspension of disbelief is a characteristic of reading fiction, for Black romance readers, that suspension has long required overlooking the absence of a diverse world in romance. Or, more important, as we see in historical romances, a hue and cry about historical accuracy where that phrase signifies whites only. For a Black historical romance reader during the late '70s and '80s, the romance genre norms were white heroes and heroines regardless of setting and time. By the '90s, Black authors were penning contemporary romance novels (Sandra Kitt and Rosalind Welles among others) and the publication of *Night Song* meant Black romance readers no longer faced the invisibility or marginalization of Black love in pre-twentieth-century historical romance. Readers of these early Black romance authors found characters whose lives were as complex and varied (professionally, socially, and nationally) as their own, calibrated according to the main tenets of the romance genre—the centrality of a love story and an emotionally satisfying ending.

As a reader/lover of historical fiction, I cannot explain what it meant to see the cover of *Night Song*. The image of a Black couple in an embrace not only told me what I could expect to find inside but also that I, a Black romance reader, mattered. Yet this moment of pleasure was tempered by the cover's nuanced appeal to a white gaze. The couple's coloring is light enough to appeal to white readers while making clear to Black readers this book is "for you." A marketing tendency that continues even now, twenty-plus years after the publication of *Night Song*. When Alyssa Cole's Loyal League series was published, the covers of these historical romance novels depicted individuals rather than couples. The visual message is an interesting one. On the one hand, the reader knows exactly what they're getting: a story line that centers a Black woman or Black man. What is left ambiguous is the telltale sign of an HEA, a couple. In many ways, the visual marketing of The Loyal League is designed, I would argue, to appeal to readers of historical fiction as much as to romance readers. When we look at other traditionally published Black-authored historical romances, the difference is notable.

Vanessa Riley's Advertisements for Love series, an interracial series of novels set in Regency England, are marked by the couple embrace. The Black women's coloring ranges from ambiguous (*The Butterfly Bride*) to dark skinned (*The Bittersweet Bride*). With the exception of Jenkins's books, Black historical romance readers are more likely to see interracial couple embraces than a Black couple embrace, or in the case of Cole's series, individual Black women and men. Clearly, desire to reach as wide a readership as possible means that the "white gaze" has to be a factor, and an interesting work-around has emerged—the illustrated cover. Riley's most recent historical romances, *A Duke, the Lady, and a Baby* and *An Earl, the Girl, and a Toddler*, reflect this trend. The mere presence of these images sends a message that some traditional publishers recognized the economic value of non-white readers even if they continue to treat the historical romance's readership as a generation of white, middle-aged, cishet women.

For this historical romance reader, the impact of Beverly Jenkins on this romance subgenre cannot be overstated. Prior to the publication of *Night Song*, it was difficult to find a historical romance novel that did not marginalize or make invisible Black and other non-white communities. That I continued to read Kathleen Woodiwiss's novels after *The Flame and the Flower* is testament to my historical romance resilience. Over the years, Jenkins has become a standard by which I measure the subgenre. Reading a Jenkins historical romance draws attention to the possibilities of historical romance to engage in world-building and characterizations that acknowledge the Black gaze. What distinguishes Jenkins's historical canon is the level of historical research she is willing to pursue to world-build. As Jenkins observes in an interview on the *Black Romance Podcast*, "So, in New

York's mind and in probably most of the country, when you write a nineteenth-century story, featuring Black people, it should center on slavery. So here I come with this story, nineteenth century, Black people, living in a small town on the plains of Kansas, and they are like 'Huh? What do we do with this?' So nobody knew what to do with it. They loved the writing, they loved the concept, but there was no box for it, even though it was romance."

What resonated with me as I listened to the interview was the pervasive sense that, even in the late twentieth century, romance publishing shared similar reading habits as the students in my Renaissance and early modern English romance class. Both were plagued by the issue of how to confront and characterize a normative that meets romance genre criteria but isn't what we expect. How do we read a historical romance that meets all our expectations for craft, conventions, and satisfying romance ending, yet not see the validity of Black or non-white representations of love? As a reader of traditionally published romances that have long centered whiteness, I had often wondered at the scarcity of historical romance novels that featured non-white couples, families, and communities. As a Black reader and an academic, I questioned the idea that, for *Night Song*, "there was no box for it" where the box clearly signals readership. Assuming that the book met all the criteria of the romance genre and the historical romance subgenre, what new "box" was needed to categorize *Night Song*?

Alyssa Cole and Vanessa Riley benefited from the "outside the box" that Jenkins's romances initiated. Both authors have nineteenth-century romances, set in the United States or Anglo-Caribbean worlds, and have received accolades for their fictions. Thus, to suggest a shift in publishing attitudes toward the viability and potential success of Black-authored historical romances is not unreasonable. The success of these authors goes beyond traditional historical romance readership demographics. Simply stated, the unambiguous popularity of these authors reflects a hunger for historical romances that speak to their desires to see themselves or other people of color at the center. Even so, Alyssa Cole's *An Extraordinary Union* (2017) was subject to a review that demonstrated white historical romance readers had a long way to go.

In a review of Cole's book on the *All About Romance* website, two white reviewers fell back on familiar and problematic terrain, historical accuracy. As one of the reviewers (SD) commented, "I, too, questioned the historical accuracy of Elle's position. And, to be very honest, I felt like her freedoms just made things too convenient for her and Malcolm." The other reviewer (EBW) considered the book "a never ending cycle of history lecture." In a comment section on the review site, EBW remarked, "Honestly, I'm confused about the praise for this book. I understand/believe this is a much underdeveloped time period and subject area in Romancelandia (and that slavery in and of itself isn't romantic), and Ms. Cole's twist—slaves as spies—is brilliant. But praising a book simply because it's a good idea when the execution is poor, is wrong." EBW also raised the historical accuracy flag: "Though I think the cover is beautiful, it isn't historically accurate & again, are we glamorizing slave life?" [Nota bene: this comment is made about the gown the cover model is wearing.] Reading this review, it becomes evident the problem has less to do with Cole's romance and more to do with the reviewers' perception of enslaved Black people. As EBW says, "I realize this is romantic fiction but I found this depiction of slave life trivialized the very real lack of independence experienced by slaves in the South."

In the end, what troubled these reviewers wasn't the romance fiction but the fact that the "historical depiction" of Elle did not adhere to their expectations and beliefs, despite SD's self-own that she does not "have a great deal of knowledge of Civil War history." What the white reviewers wanted wasn't an interracial historical romance set during the US Civil War period. As SD's comments make clear—"I would have liked to see Malcolm woo Elle a bit, which would have made their relationship more believable" or "I think it was a bit too idealistic. It would be wonderful if everyone was super accepting of everyone else, but that isn't true today and it certainly wasn't true in the 1860's"—what *An Extraordinary Union* isn't is a version of "historical accuracy" that has made "plantation romances" so popular. It isn't *Gone with the Wind*.

My point here is that these are the readers traditional publishing pivots to when seeking out new historical romance projects, not Black or non-white romance readers seeking far more diversity in the subgenre. The underlying message to Black romance authors and readers in particular, but also to all non-white romance readers and authors, is obvious. If your historical romance doesn't center a specific mythology—medieval knights,

Georgette Heyer Regency-esque worlds, or in the case of the United States, white supremacist expectations about the viability of non-white love relationships—it won't sell. If it doesn't fit a "box" . . .

My frustration at the sparsity of Black historical romances, especially those set in early historical periods (medieval, early modern, antiquity), has not stopped me from being an avid Black reader of historical romances, as my eclectic reading habits acquired as a child remain fully intact. I am as enamored of Katrina Jackson's *Office Hours* or Francis Ray's *Only You* or Rebekah Weatherspoon's *Harbor* as I am of Riley's *The Bewildered Bride* or Cole's *Agnes Moor's Wild Knight* or Jenkins's *Indigo*. In a world tainted by the celebration of whiteness, it has become a deep-seeded intellectual and personal pleasure to immerse myself in a romance novel where Black women and men are centered, where Black trauma isn't the sole purpose of the novel, and where a happily ever after is not an afterthought.

Writing Black Romance

Writing has always been a necessary element in my life, yet I did not complete my first romance manuscript until I was in my mid-thirties. The memory remains vivid because I wrote my dissertation during the day and my historical romance at night. Writing romance was solace, a way to distance myself from the academic world that reminded me daily that I was a Black woman fighting for a place in a specialized literary field, largely masculine and predominately white. The romance work in progress was set during the sixteenth century and my heroine traveled to England in search of her sibling. It was an interracial romance and it was badly written. I never submitted that manuscript; even I understood that I would need to master the craft of fiction writing. As an undergraduate and a graduate student, I had taken creative writing courses. At the time, I found my creative writing classes informative and painful. I had no desire to become a poet or dramatist. I voiced my desire to pursue fiction, specifically romance and historical genres. My instructors often denigrated romance fiction and unequivocally referred to romance as "genre" or "trash" fiction and not where I should focus my efforts. Poetry and literary fiction were the writer's "gods" and that was where I should set my goals. So I stopped taking classes and my manuscript languished on my computer, neglected and eventually forgotten beneath the weight of an academic career and publications.

I retired from teaching and focused on a new career path, or a return to an old career path, writing romance fiction. In 2015, my first historical work in progress received recognition in a national contest, and the full manuscript was requested by a publishing editor. The acquiring editor's praise for the manuscript's writing and world-building was a balm to my soul. Impostor syndrome is quite real. What was devastating was the request to set the story two centuries later because then it potentially could be marketed. Since then, I have received mixed signals from traditional publishing acquisition editors who find my world-building engaging yet are unable to relate to the characters or want a different time period. I continued to work on craft and, when it was complete, the manuscript that became *Fate's Consort* was requested. Almost immediately, the acquiring editor asked whether the story line could be recast as a ménage/taboo situation. The plot is a paranormal romance, the main characters are a Black female supernatural and an angelic pair of twins. In the pitch, there was nothing to indicate that the story line was a ménage. I considered the acquiring editor's request an insult and refused, and the editor sent an email stating she couldn't "relate" to the characters or the story.

Even more problematic were the requests for full manuscripts and then dead silence from the acquiring editors. In 2018, I pitched my then manuscript, *Your Heart Only*. It is a contemporary Black romance whose tropes include a secret baby and a marriage of convenience. When I pitched the manuscript, two acquiring editors seemed enthusiastic about it, especially the plot twist on Shakespeare's sonnet 130 ("My Mistress' Eyes"). I submitted the manuscript. The silence has been ongoing now for nearly three years. In the end, dear reader, after these experiences with traditional publishing, I chose the self-publishing path.

One of the pleasures of being a Black romance author is I write books I want to read and, hopefully, other Black readers will want to read—romances filled with characters who reflect the range of intersectional lives of family members, friends, and professional colleagues. I write characters who are sword-wielding warriors, courtesans, Shakespearean professors, innkeepers, shape-shifters and angels, lawyers, actors, elementary school teachers, and spies. All are African-descended. Some will be gender fluid, some will not. What all my characters have in common is their humanness and capacity to love, to find their happily ever after in an often openly hostile world because of racism.

Like many Black romance authors, I have found my community of writers. One of the most important people in my circle is Mia Heintzelman. Mia writes contemporary interracial romance (rom-com and dark) whereas I am all over the generic map. She was an early and critical reader of each version of *Your Heart Only*, reading drafts and "checking" my academic tendency to write prosaic, long-winded sentences. As a Black romance author and reader, Mia became a trusted beta reader/critique partner whose opinion I highly value. This partnership makes it easier to navigate the romance publishing industry, the self-doubts, and the implicit and explicit racial microaggressions Black romance authors often face within the romance community—whether from publishers, readers, or reviewers. With each published book, I find it easier to write stories that center Black women, Black love, and Black histories in all their complexity without pandering to a problematic white gaze. Without question, Black women and men face obstacles and it is those obstacles that make for a rich story line. Marisa Price, the heroine of *Your Heart Only*, has to deal with an abusive ex who is out to destroy her academic career, but in Aidan Graywolf, she finds a Black man who desires and comes to love her as a partner because of her strength, her love for their daughter, and her trust in him. The heroines of my Daughters of Saria paranormal series are fierce warriors of African descent who have to confront the history of enslavement and genetic manipulation of African-born or -descended peoples to stop a supernatural civil war. These are women who love and are loved by the men in their lives. More important, these are Black women who wear their identities proudly. None are conflicted about who they are as Black women, which is so important to me as an author and a reader.

Black romance readers are varied in their reading across generic lines. Yet what all these Black readers have in common is a love of romance fiction and a need to have Black voices tell the stories of Black lives and love. Too often, we are offered romances that either replicate racist ideologies about Black people (trauma, deprivation, and the need for saviors, always white) or present Black characters as repositories for white guilt. While I would not categorically state that non-Black authors are incapable of writing Black romances, it is a rare non-Black author who is fully capable of moving past the illogic of white supremacist ideologies about Black communities and therefore Black relationships. What is not rare is being told that Blackness is a romance liability, especially in historical romances, especially those set outside the context of the United States and its complicated racial histories.

Two novels, one romance and the other "speculative fiction," played an important role in my romance writing: Alyssa Cole's *Agnes Moor's Wild Knight* and Octavia Butler's *Wild Seed*. Cole's novella affirmed my decision to write historical romances set between 1580 and 1700 when I searched for more examples and found none. So much of the academic research underlying my nonfiction publications centers on this period of time. It was easy to build on this world, creating characters—Black and white, non-Black and mixed race—whose lives mirrored or tangentially touched the untold histories of early modern England's diverse population.

Wild Seed influenced the supernatural characterization of Amina in *Fate's Match* and Anne Willoughby in *Fate's Kiss*. Both characters are fictional descendants of two historical African-born or descended women. Amina's historical source was an enslaved woman called "the Negress Maria" by the white men who claimed her. Historical accounts do not give us her African name. Anne Willoughby, the heroine of *Fate's Kiss*, is based on a mid-seventeenth-century Black courtesan, Mary Neale. The final two books of the Daughters of Saria series, *Fate's Consort* and *Fate's Promise*, continue the genealogy of historical paranormal romance. In adapting Book I of John Milton's *Paradise Lost*, I found it easier to redirect our readerly gaze and challenge presumptions about history, about Black women, and about the havoc whiteness can wreak on marginalized lives. The female protagonist of *Fate's Consort* and *Fate's Promise*, Analise Saria Willoughby, lives in a world of humans and supernaturals, and she is Fate. It was a pleasure to write Fate as a Black woman, to consider how intersectionality can shape not just my reading of romance but my writing romance as well. Analise is the culmination of my generic experimentations in *Fate's Match* and *Fate's Kiss*. Yet—and this is the joy in being a Black romance reader—Analise carries within her "romance DNA" the codes of my love for contemporary Black romance authors (far too many to name here, but Melissa Blue, Francis Ray, Delaney Diamond, Farrah Rochon, Brenda Jackson, and Christina C. Jones are some authors who have me seriously fangirling).

As a Black romance author, I have been fortunate in my literary life. I have the ability to write the happily ever after I want to read. I do not have to cater to a white gaze to see my books into the world. My books are first and foremost intended for Black and other non-white readers. They are stories that reflect the joy, the love, and the possibilities of forever relationships between and involving Black people. With each book, I am increasingly aware of the diverse spectrum of readers and potential readers. And like any politically committed romance author, I look at how I represent that spectrum. I am also aware that writing historical romances (my current romance work in progress is set in Elizabeth I's court and my protagonists are Black sisters) means I will engage in a degree of "historical inaccuracy" for the story line while also not erasing aspects of English histories steeped in white supremacy. What this also means is the views of historical romance readers who want "authenticity" in the representation of the past don't matter. These readers, mostly white, are not my intended audience. As a Black romance author, I write for Black and other non-white readers. Readers aware that depictions of "historical accuracy" in the romance genre is a subset of white supremacy.

My romance novels are not for the readers who declare, "I realize this is romantic fiction but I found this depiction of slave life trivialized the very real lack of independence experienced by slaves in the South." This reader, and other pearl clutchers about historical authenticity, are not important to the romance stories I want to put into the world. As someone who has spent time in historical archives, I find the idea of historical accuracy not just problematic but also a facile assumption when it comes to histories and the depiction of the past. Similarly, the question of "relatability" is also unimportant to me as a romance author. I do not ask my readers to "relate" to my characters but to follow their journeys to a happily ever after. What is important to me, as a Black romance author, is to give my readers historical stories that center Black lives and Black romance.

I joined the romance community as an adult, yet inside this romance author and reader remains that young Black girl growing up in a segregated California community filled with examples of Black love. Although that young girl initially had no dreams of becoming a romance author and a Shakespeare and early modern English professor, she never stopped reading and became all three. I do wish I still had that library card.

Food of Love

JASMINE GUILLORY

T here's so much food in this book!"

That comment—one I've consistently gotten on all my books since my first, *The Wedding Date*—has always bemused me, especially at the beginning. At first I didn't really understand it: I write romance novels; of course there's a lot of food in my books! Doesn't everyone show love through food?

Well, apparently not, but my characters all do. And, I've realized, they do so because my family—especially the elders in my family—modeled this to me throughout my life. Cooking someone's favorite dish for them, cooking your own favorite dish to share with them, making sure someone is well nourished and well taken care of—those are some of the many ways my grandparents taught me how to show love.

Granny and Papa—my father's parents—had what I now realize was a pretty small house, when you consider they had eight children and seventeen grandchildren. But it never felt small to me. We all crowded into the living room, where Granny's stories were always on the television, and Papa always rocked in his rocking chair and pretended he wasn't paying attention to them. We all played in the backyard, fighting and making up and having constant adventures every day. And we all spent a lot of time in Granny's kitchen. There were always cookies in the cookie jar, Popsicles in the freezer, and often gumbo on the stove. But the thing I remember more than any other that Granny made was her coconut cake. She made it for every event, every birthday, every holiday, and though I don't even really like coconut cake, I always ate it. Once, in my early twenties—when Papa was gone, and Granny was fading—I said something to one of my older cousins about that coconut cake, and how it was Granny's favorite cake. My cousin laughed and said, "No, that was Papa's favorite cake."

All that time, Granny had really been making the cake for Papa. I hadn't even realized it. Granny and Papa were never particularly affectionate with one another, or with us, their grandchildren, even though none of us have ever doubted how much they loved us. And maybe this is one reason why: they always both found a way to show us—and each other—their love in other ways.

My Grandma—my mother's mom—had three husbands, all of whom she loved dearly. She and my grandfather—her first husband—got divorced when my mother was little, but they remained best friends until my grandfather died, and they talked on the phone almost every day. (I sometimes wonder what their subsequent spouses thought of their relationship; knowing my grandmother, their opinions would not have mattered to her at all.) They didn't see each other that often—they got divorced for a reason—but Grandma would sometimes drop food over at his house, just to make sure he was eating right.

Her third husband, Stan, was another grandfather to me. When I think of him, I think of the many ways he showed me that he loved me—his great pride in my accomplishments, how he found me my first car, how he would wear my college and law school sweatshirts everywhere, just for an opportunity to brag about me. But those aren't the things I think of most. I think of him every time I fry myself an egg in butter, like he used to make for me. I think of him every time I make, or have, red beans and rice, just like he used to make, from his native New Orleans. And I think of him, and of my grandmother, and how much they loved each other, whenever I do one very specific kitchen task.

When Stan was dying, he came home from the hospital for his last few days. I came over to the house to see him, for what I thought might be—and was—the last time I saw him. When I walked into the house that afternoon, my grandmother was at the kitchen table, peeling and deveining shrimp. I said, "Grandma, what are you doing?" She snapped at me, in a way that didn't hurt my feelings at all, "I'm peeling and deveining shrimp!" I said, "Yes, but . . . why?" She said, "Well, people still have to eat lunch!"

I just smiled and went to the back room, where Stan's hospital bed had been set up. He was totally lucid, in good spirits, and was smiling and joking with me as usual. And then he asked me, "What's your grandmother doing?" I said, "She's peeling and deveining shrimp." He looked at me, and I looked back at him, and we both burst out laughing. That shared, joyous laughter, at my grandmother and her ways, ways that we both found exasperating and loved at the same time, is my last memory of Stan. It's a really great one.

I learned this lesson from my grandmothers, more or less unconsciously. When I love someone—or even like them a lot—I want to feed them. And not just any food: I want to feed them food that they'll love, food that will nourish their soul. I want to share meals with people, cook for them in times of joy and in times of sorrow. In law school, when I was first becoming friends with the group of people who, many years later, are still some of my closest friends in the world, I made jambalaya for them all in my tiny grad-student kitchen. I'd never made it without my mom in the kitchen with me; I burned myself taking the pan out of the oven (I still have the faint scars of that burn), and it was a really great night.

Whenever something good or bad happens to loved ones who are far away, my first goal is to find a way to get them food I know will make them happy. One of my best friends had a difficult pregnancy, and one of the few foods that comforted her during that hard time were chocolate chip cookies from a specific bakery near her house. When she had the baby, I couldn't go to see her, because I was on the other side of the country. But another friend and I conspired to get a delivery of a dozen of the cookies to her hospital room. She still remembers those cookies, what a surprise they were, and how loved they made her feel. And years after I made that jambalaya, when one of those same law school friends had a family emergency, I baked brownies and shipped them to him and his family. I couldn't do anything to help them in the way I wished I could, but I hoped they could feel the love in those brownies.

One of the things I missed so much during the pandemic was being able to cook for people I love. Even though it was hard, I found small ways to do it. A friend had a baby early in the pandemic, and I brought cinnamon rolls to her house—I left them in a bag outside the front door, and then she stood at the window and held the baby up to me, and we waved and smiled while her older daughter feasted. A friend's mother passed away a few months into the pandemic—my friend couldn't be with her mom, I couldn't be with my friend, and I ached for her and her loss. I sent her half a dozen pints of gourmet ice cream, in the hopes that the food could show her, a little, how much I love her and mourned for her.

One sad, precious moment from that year was from when a friend's beloved dog died. She lives near me, and so when I saw her post about the dog, I immediately made cookies to bring to her house. She opened the door, saw the cookies, and started crying. Then she put her mask on, and said, "Can we hug?" That was one of the best hugs I've ever had.

And when loved ones do this for me, it touches me deeply. A few years ago, three weeks before my first book came out, I had my own, compounded, family emergency, with two family members on the same critical floor of the same hospital. When a far-away friend texted me a $5 Starbucks gift card and told me to get a treat with it, it made me cry (I still tear up when I think about it). When, in the midst of the pandemic, I reached a small but meaningful personal milestone, two friends surprised me with a hand-delivered cheesecake. When, relatively early in our relationship, an ex began to bring me coffee every morning, with the exact amount of milk and sugar I like in it, I started to fall in love.

I am also endlessly fascinated by food, and the kinds of food we love and the kinds of food we share with one another, and I think it can say a lot about who a person—or a fictional character—is. Whenever there's a description in a book or show of a meal where something major happens to characters, I always want to know what they're eating. (The Friday night dinners in *Gilmore Girls* never had quite enough details about the food for my taste.) I've always gravitated toward books that are specific about the food and drinks involved, and those scenes always seemed to sparkle for me. Is there anyone out there who read *Anne of Green Gables* who didn't want to have some of that "raspberry cordial" that got Anne drunk? If so, I haven't met them.

So of course it feels natural to me that when two people are attracted to one another, they'd share cheese and crackers; that a gift of early-morning doughnuts would cause a woman's heart to beat faster; that flirting over a table full of tacos would be a perfect first date; and that a winning manner of courtship would be a cake delivery—not of just any cake, but the exact cake someone said she loves. Gifts of food can do so much, both for the recipient and the giver. They're a way to share part of yourself, a way to nourish someone else, to give them a treat, either as a celebration or a pick-me-up when they need it. And they also make someone feel seen, cared for, and loved. Food is the way to my heart, in real life as well as in fiction.

Black Cultural Studies and Black Love

Why Black Love Matters

JULIE E. MOODY-FREEMAN

Black love matters because it has sustained African and Black diasporic peoples through the relentless physical and emotional assaults on Black humanity and through times when all has seemed hopeless. In this period of my life, this mantra has come to be my mission. It guides what I read, teach, research, and creatively produce. I wasn't always consciously focused on this mission, however. I happened upon it because of my life experiences and through a critical race practice that examines and challenges media and popular culture representations of Black people as not loving or incapable of being loved.

I am a Literature and Cultural Studies scholar who teaches and publishes on Black love and Black romance. I created, produce, and host the *Black Romance Podcast*, which I developed in 2020 to build an oral history on Black writers' and editors' experiences writing and publishing in the romance industry.

How I got to this point can only be explained by amazing synchronicity.

Reading Tales in a Central American British Colony

My early reading habits could not have predicted my current work in Black love and Black romance. Growing up as a young Black woman in a British colony, my early education was steeped in British culture, history, and society. For all intents and purposes, there is no way I could have imagined doing what I am doing now. I was born in Belize, Central America, and grew up in Belize when it was still a British colony. I was about five years old when Belize was granted self-government, and it wasn't until I was in high school that Belize became an independent country, in 1981. Because Belize was a British colony, before I got to high school, most of the books I read for class or for fun featured white characters from Europe and the United States. My favorite library was a short distance from my primary school, so on my way home, I would stock up on The Adventure Series by English writer Enid Blyton and *Pippi Longstocking* by Astrid Lindgren, a Swedish writer. My grand-aunt and godmother, Mrs. Alma Hinkson, who was a principal, would help me to build my tiny personal library with precious adventure books by Blyton, which I loved, and with others from Ladybird Books, based in London.

With the rare exception of *Roots*—read to us in Standard Five by Mrs. Usher, who wanted us to know about Black history—and secondhand *Ebony* and *Jet* magazines that we occasionally received from the United States, the books I read centered around white experiences, history, culture, and societies. My first two years of high school I did not read books with Black characters. Academically, my teachers prepared some of us in our second year for the Royal Society of Arts exams in English and literature, so we read books by British writers. For fun, I, along with a few high school friends, snuck and read our mothers' romance novels. Overhearing my mom talking to a neighbor about a book she was reading, I secretly read it. I have no recollection of the characters' names or the plot, but it was a Mills & Boon novel, which were so popular that every romance novel, regardless of the publisher, was called Mills & Boon. My best friend would also let me borrow novels written by Dame Barbara Cartland, who wrote historical novels mostly set in the Victorian period. My friend borrowed them from her mom, who allowed her to read them because they were "clean" books; i.e., the heroines were all virgins until marriage.

The love stories and the happily ever after (HEA) endings lured me back to the Mills & Boon and Barbara Cartland novels repeatedly. Reading love stories with HEA endings by white writers became a common practice from my final years in high school in Belize to graduate school in North Carolina.

Discovering Black Romance Fiction in the United States

In the United States, romance novels were great distractions from my graduate work and feelings of loneliness because I was far away from my family. I could get lost in the novels' various settings and hosts of characters: knights, lords, football heroes, and Scottish lairds. I loved the novels by Jude Deveraux, Johanna Lindsey, Betina Krahn, Julie Garwood, Susan Elizabeth Phillips, Lisa Kleypas, and Lynn Kurland. It didn't matter what these writers published; I would read everything. I especially enjoyed the medieval romances and time travel novels, but it didn't matter if some of these writers' settings were contemporary or historical. It never concerned me that the characters were white. I didn't read the novels because I aspired to become white. I didn't lack or lose self-esteem because I read books with characters who were white. The joy of reading romance was about the paths characters would take to discover love and receive their happy endings.

While reading romance novels, I had in grad school discovered and had simultaneously been reading several Black writers, including James Baldwin, Toni Morrison, Alice Walker, Gloria Naylor, and Octavia Butler. I loved all these writers, but the strong romantic elements in Gloria Naylor's *Mama Day* made that book my favorite. That was the first time I was introduced to an amazing love story between two Black characters. Of course the happy ending was missing for George and Cocoa, but there was enough romance in it for me to return to it repeatedly and find ways to incorporate it into several syllabi when I began teaching college students in the late 1990s.

Reading Octavia Butler's *Wild Seed* provided me with the romantic elements and what I saw as Black characters who had a happy ending. In *Wild Seed*, Butler's depiction of Doro and

Anyanwu's relationship resembled an epic and paranormal romance, which I eventually loved reading years later in Elysabeth Grace's novels from her Daughters of Saria series. In *Wild Seed*, I enjoyed reading about the two Black protagonists with fantastic abilities and powers who were drawn to each other. Read as a stand-alone book, the novel had an HEA since Anyanwu discovered Doro's true essence, and Doro shared with her who he was without doing what came natural to him, killing. Although this book was not technically a popular romance novel, it contained enough romantic elements for me. The ending satisfied my insatiable desire for happy endings with characters who loved each other.

It was not until I had almost completed graduate school in the United States that I discovered popular romance novels with Black characters. In passing, I mentioned to one of my thesis advisers that I loved reading romance, but I wished that I could read romance with Black characters like myself. She told me that somebody had just started publishing romance novels with Black characters. I went on the hunt for those novels and that began my journey. During the 1990s, I fell in love with books from Sandra Kitt, Francis Ray, Brenda Jackson, Rochelle Alers, Donna Hill, Shirley Hailstock, Eboni Snoe, and Felicia Mason.

While I worked on my graduate degree in Literature and Cultural Studies, I read the "acceptable" literary fiction by day and romance by white and Black writers at night and on weekends. I kept the two reading practices separate. The first set of books were for my career while the latter were for enjoyment. I literally kept them hidden in a closet, even as I studiously kept up with the Black romance writers published by Kensington, BET, St. Martin's Press, and Harlequin.

Discovering and Teaching an Ethic of Love

While I had been reading love stories for entertainment, I had not thought much about love or what it meant. I happened upon bell hooks's books on love in the early 2000s, while working on a project on Black intellectuals. The clear language and definitions she provided helped me to begin to articulate and evaluate what love meant. For me, a couple of chapters of her book *All About Love* were impactful. In chapter one, "Clarity: Give Love Words," hooks defines love and suggests that we think of love as a verb rather than how it is traditionally used as a "feeling." Next, she argues, "To truly love we must learn to mix various ingredients—care, affection, recognition, respect, commitment, and trust, as well as honest and open communication." In chapter two, "Justice: Childhood Love Lessons," these statements struck me as useful: "Love and abuse cannot coexist." She posits, "Loving parents work hard to discipline without punishment . . . They focus on teaching children how to be self-disciplining and how to take control for their actions." My son was still a toddler, so *All About Love* helped me to think about how to put "love in action," as hooks articulated it. I began incorporating this ethic of love in my parenting practices using her definition of love and her ideas about raising "self-disciplining" children who could make decisions without fear of punishment.

I engaged with bell hooks's ethic of love on a personal level, but I became an advocate for an ethic of Black love to be taught in the classroom after watching Henry Louis Gates, Jr.'s 2004 PBS series *America Beyond the Color Line*. In one episode, Arnon Milchan, the producer of *Daredevil*, *Pretty Woman*, *Brazil*, and *Free Willy*, told Gates that "white people aren't interested in watching black people fall in love and make love" (quoted in Esensten). In the documentary, Milchan argues, "People don't like to see a black woman and black man even going to bed . . . Russell Crowe and Halle Berry yes . . . no different than Whitney Houston and Kevin Costner." You could have seen my jaw drop during these revelations. Living in the United States for sixteen years, I had seen and experienced racism. However, to hear Milchan's assessment of the industry and viewers expressed so candidly and so matter-of-factly took me by surprise. I was sad and angry at the same time. How could anyone think of Black people like me as unlovable or incapable of giving love? My first thought turned to students in my class, and I immediately knew that I needed to develop a class on Black love.

Deciding to develop and teach a course on Black love was scary, but I was determined to uncover the antipathy to Black love and to make sure the students who entered my classroom received an intellectual grounding that would lead to an affinity with the history, literature, and culture of Black people. I was one year into a tenure-track position in a newly established African and Black Diaspora Studies Program (ABD). I, along with a colleague, had been hired to teach in such a newly minted program that the courses we developed would shape the curriculum. It was exciting and scary at the same time. The chair of the program, a Black philosopher, often dropped by my office to check up on me. He stopped by shortly after I had seen the documentary. I told him about it and then hesitatingly, even laughingly, told him I wanted to teach a class on Black love. I used the word *hesitatingly* because I actually thought he would dismiss my proposal as drivel and unintellectual because the focus would be on love. However, his response was immediate enthusiasm, and he suggested we call it Blacks and Love. I developed the syllabus, put together a proposal for it to earn Liberal Studies Domain credit, and taught ABD 220: Blacks and Love for the first time in summer 2005. My chair continued to be supportive of the course and even organized a Black Love symposium.

In the course, I approached the study of Blacks and love by interrogating the denigration of Blackness and studying varying articulations of an ethic of love grounded in Black philosophy and Black feminist theory. I employed cultural criticism, race and ethnic studies, and women's and gender studies to examine the visual representations of Blacks and love in art, film, and literature. The course began by examining the construction of race in eighteenth-, nineteenth-, and early-twentieth-century European and American philosophy and body politic and with an examination of art, art history, film, and literature.

In the first two weeks, I opened the class with a discussion of race and white supremacy grounded in historical context with discussions of racial scientists like Arthur de Gobineau and Thomas Jefferson's views on slavery and Blacks in *Notes on the State of Virginia* (1784–1785). I used examples that clearly referred to Jefferson's views on Black love. About slaves, Jefferson asserts: "Their [Black slaves,] love is ardent, but it kindles the senses only, not the imagination." He also posits: "They are more ardent after their female; But love seems with them to be more an eager desire, than a tender delicate mixture of sentiment and sensation." Jefferson's conclusions have had lasting repercussions for African Americans: "In general, their existence appears to participate more of sensation than reflection." Following the class discussion of Gobineau and Jefferson, we examine why Black love matters in a society shaped by anti-Black racism that's embedded in laws, policies, literature, media, and culture. For this, I used hooks's *Salvation: Black People and Love*. In *Salvation*, hooks draws on the work of Martin Luther King, Jr., and the feminist theoretical foundation developed in her early works. hooks encourages Black people to radically examine their duplication of a "dominant white supremacist capitalist patriarchal" way of thinking and being in this world. She urges Black people to reject this way of thinking and being and to choose the challenging task of loving themselves and building a healthy love ethic in Black families, in Black communities, and in national and global politics. Through the course of *Salvation*, it becomes clear that, for hooks, several requirements are necessary for a return to a love ethic that involves Black self-love. For her, Black people must come to understand the negative forces of oppression that lead to a denigration of Blackness, the "desolation of the spirit," and the subsequent loss of a love ethic in their personal lives, families, and communities. They must also reject these negative forces, which will lead to a love of self. Self-loving Black people can accomplish a more integrated approach to ending oppressions globally. To accomplish this return to a love ethic in Black communities, hooks argues that first Black people must reject negative images of Blackness and decolonize their minds to resist white supremacist thinking.

I used bell hooks's books *All About Love* and *Salvation: Black People and Love* as the framing texts for ABD 220: Blacks and Love. While *All About Love* provided the definitions I used in the class, *Salvation: Black People and Love* helped me to thoroughly explore how to apply her definition of love to the particular historical and cultural context of Black people in the United States. I also included excerpts from Martin Luther King, Jr.'s *Strength to Love*. Both *All About Love* and *Salvation* demonstrate the profound impact King has had on hooks's writings, particularly on the "synthesis of love and justice," a fusing of "word and deed" and "love in action." hooks's writings on Black people and love reflect King's love ethic. Since hooks and King are writing in different historical contexts, love as activism takes on different ideological forms. Therefore, students and I spent time analyzing hooks's and King's writings for the similarities and differences. Other works studied in this class over the years include: Harriet Jacobs's *Incidents in the Life of a Slave Girl*; *Love and Marriage in Early African America*; Charles W. Chesnutt's "The Wife of His Youth"; Darnell L. Moore's "What Freedom Feels Like: On Love, Empathy, and Pleasure in the Age of Neoliberalism"; Michael Eric Dyson's *Why I Love Black Women*; Alexis DeVeaux's "Bird of Paradise"; Langston Hughes's "Blessed Assurance"; Audre Lorde's "Man Child" and "Uses of the Erotic" from *Sister Outsider*; Becky Birtha's "In the

Life"; Brenda Jackson's "Strictly Business"; and *Love Jones*, among others.

Reactions to the Class on Black Love

Reactions to this course were generally positive, but one suggestion offered by an older well-meaning Black faculty member almost derailed my resolve. This course was popular when I taught it in the early 2000s and remains popular when I teach it today. It is always guaranteed to be fully enrolled, and students from all races and cultural backgrounds love this class. However, a Black woman, a full professor who had been at the institution several decades, cautioned me about teaching a course called Blacks and Love. She advised me to change the title of the course to something like Black Families. She cautioned that this was best for students because the title of my course wouldn't look good listed on students' transcripts. I cannot speculate about her motivations. What I can attest to is how debilitating her perspective was for me. It amplified whatever apprehensions I had myself. The self-doubt I had about teaching a course on love reared its head. I guess I thought about how people would perceive me and a class like this. Perhaps they would think of it as lacking rigor. I had not come up for tenure yet, so those comments really bothered me. I briefly stopped teaching the course, but after much reflection, I returned Blacks and Love to the rotation of courses I taught every year.

This class was so much more important than intellectual respectability politics, so, after licking my wounds, I came back with a more defiant iteration of the course. I no longer began the course with Arthur de Gobineau or Thomas Jefferson. Instead, I examined Black philosophical and literary writings that challenge theories of Blacks as unloving. It explored Christian and secular definitions of love as well as concepts of love shaped by Black political thought and feminist theory. Further, it theorized about the interconnection between love, race, power, and justice. Students' final projects drew on the works of bell hooks, Martin Luther King, Jr., Darnell L. Moore, Audre Lorde, June Jordan, and Michael Eric Dyson to argue how a cultural or political work illustrates the practice of Black love.

This tale of teaching a course on Blacks and love ends happily ever after. I received tenure with the class listed on my curriculum vitae. Furthermore, students have gone on to graduate programs, law school, teaching, and professional careers with nary an issue about a course on their transcript titled Blacks and Love.

Black Romance: Lessons in Black Love

In a society whose history is steeped in Black trauma, and one that has profited from enslaved Black bodies in labor and in pain, I feel that it is imperative that I center my teaching, research, writing, and podcasting on Black love and Black romance. When I teach my classes, I want students to understand the history of Black love that has sustained Black people when all seemed hopeless. Every time I teach Harriet Jacobs's *Incidents in the Life of a Slave Girl* (1861), I am reminded of this. Sometimes we are so overwhelmed by images of the horrors of slavery that we fail to recognize the actions of the enslaved that illustrate the care and love Blacks had for each other. Reading Jacobs's autobiography, I try not to become so overwhelmed by her account of Mr. Flint and his wife's inhumane treatment of her that I miss the moments when she offers glimpses of how enslaved Black people like herself loved. In spite of her enslaver's power over her body and freedom, Jacobs meets his attempt to dominate her with defiance and subterfuge. Jacobs remains in love with a free Black man in spite of her enslaver. We read of Jacobs (named Linda Brent in the autobiography) wanting to marry a young Black carpenter who was born free. She is prevented from marrying him because her enslaver, Mr. Flint, refuses to allow it. Out of love for her lover and a desire to see him safe, she asks him to leave and go live in a free state where he cannot be touched by slavery. In addition, Jacobs offers us glimpses of her loving relationship with her brother. Jacobs's narrative emphasizes the love and affection they have for each other. The brother tenderly looks into Harriet's eyes to discern how she is feeling, and they lovingly hug to provide comfort to each other.

Incidents illustrates that even in slavery, love exists in spaces where Black people are present. However, those spaces are guarded at all costs by enslaved people like Jacobs for fear that their love for each other could be used against them for profit and to mete out pain. The narrative emphasizes how Jacobs hides her love for her brother from her enslaver so that he is not wrenched from her life. This approach to teaching Jacobs's autobiography reflects what Treva B. Lindsey, Black feminist and author of *Colored No More: Reinventing Black Womanhood in Washington, D.C.*, articulates as a meaningful way to "hold trauma and pleasure" and "holding them in productive tension."

Black love remains central to my academic work and to my personal life. This means I teach and write about love in literature and cultural works written and created by Black people. I read romance novels for pleasure. However, for years I kept my romance novels literally hidden in a closet. Romance was for pleasure. I didn't want it to be work. I suspect going up for tenure, I didn't want it to seem that I was studying something frivolous and not rigorous. This must have been a subconscious thought. I can't remember this being at the forefront of my mind. My more conscious thought was that analyzing romance novels would ruin my pleasure, and I wasn't about to let the academy get in the way of that. I have come to realize over the years that my academic teaching and research, though laborious, is pleasure.

My scholarly publications now focus on romance novels that feature love stories with Black characters. I have expanded my academic work to begin to develop an archive devoted to Black romance. The project began in 2020 when I created the *Black Romance Podcast*. The podcast is an oral history that documents the narratives of Black writers and editors discussing their experiences in the publishing industry. In my conversations with them during both seasons of the podcast, I have come to see their works as labors of love. I am struck by writers' and editors' insistence and persistence to publish love stories with Black characters against all odds. Their hope-filled novels with happily ever after endings for Black people remind me of bell hooks's argument that for Black people, "love is our hope." hooks affirms that "love is always there—nothing can keep us from love if we dare to seek it and to treasure what we find. Even when we cannot change ongoing exploitation and domination love gives life meaning, purpose, and direction." I offer to a present and future generation my writings and podcast as love letters attesting to a legacy of loving Black people.

Please, Sir, Can I Have Some More

How Bread Crumbs of Queer Characters in Entertainment Helped Me Establish My Own Sense of Self

KOSOKO JACKSON

I knew I was gay from an early age, but I didn't have any idea what gay was.

I think a lot of people have some great "come to Jesus" moment of their homosexuality. Something epic like a first boy they had a crush on, or some girl who made them feel a certain or specific way. I don't really have any of that. Nothing to write home about, at least. Mine is far simpler, but at the same time, twofold. In fact, it completely makes sense when I look back on it and think about who I am as a person.

I knew I was gay thanks to anime first, and live-action TV second.

The first realization came from watching an anime show

called *Mobile Fighter G Gundam*. During a scene that, like anime, is repeated over and over again, the main character, Domon Kasshu, went through this transformation that made his ass look amazing in this spandex-like black suit. I remember, when discussing the show with my friends, fixating a lot on how great that transformation was and how much I liked it. The other boys kind of looked at me weirdly and were like, "I don't really remember that," and we shrugged it off and went on to talk about something else; I can't even remember now. I was eleven then.

The second realization came when watching *Degrassi: The Next Generation*. I think a lot more gay kids can relate to this one than the first one. During this time period, there were hardly any positive gay representations on TV, so it was a huge surprise to me when I found one in the show. Now, it's important to know that when this show was on, I didn't exactly know what being gay was. I knew I had something inside me that was different, and I had, of course, heard what gay was, but I didn't think that was me, nor did I relate to it.

But that show changed my life. Not the whole show, mind you, a specific episode. Season 3, episode 4, funnily enough titled "Pride Part 1." In this episode, one of the characters, Marco Del Rossi, played by Adamo Ruggiero, comes out to his best friend, Spinner, who, of course, does not take it well. This was the first episode of Degrassi I saw, and it was a formative episode. Why, might you ask? Not only because in 2003, there, again, wasn't much gay rep, but because of this interaction at the end of the episode that I stumbled upon, sitting on the living room floor while my parents cleaned the kitchen:

> **SPINNER:** [Spinner confronts Marco in an alleyway] What are you doing?
>
> **MARCO DEL ROSSI:** Leave me alone, Spin.
>
> **SPINNER:** You just walked out on your date with Hazel. She's sitting there and . . .
>
> **MARCO DEL ROSSI:** I mean it, Spin! Please, back off!
>
> **SPINNER:** [throws Marco against a dumpster] What's going on?
>
> **MARCO DEL ROSSI:** You don't understand!
>
> **SPINNER:** That you're a psycho? You walked out on a date with one of Degrassi's coolest girls for your mom's pasta sauce? It doesn't make sense!
>
> **MARCO DEL ROSSI:** Yes, it does!
>
> **SPINNER:** Oh, yeah. Well, stop crying and explain it to me 'cause obviously I'm a moron and don't get it.
>
> **MARCO DEL ROSSI:** Because, Spin!
>
> **SPINNER:** Because what?
>
> **MARCO DEL ROSSI:** Because I'm gay.

Roll credits.

This scene might seem a little melodramatic now—and that would be because it was—but it was a groundbreaking scene back then. There was very little gay rep on TV, especially for *the youths*.

I remember sitting there, feeling like all these pieces had come together. This was real, this was me. I was exactly where I was supposed to be now. Going to let the light shine on me.

It took me a while to come to terms with what that meant. Why I liked Domon Kasshu so much. Why the scene with Marco spoke to me so much. Why I felt awkward around boys and hated their *social engagements* and had so many girlfriends, even as an eleven-year-old.

But once I figured it out, it all clicked, and it all made sense. I was gay. Like, really really gay.

As I mentioned a few sentences above, there wasn't much gay rep for teens. Even now, we still don't see a great amount of it. Only roughly 9 percent of characters in TV recognize themselves as being LGBT. That number has gone up 5 percent since 2012, which is great, yes. But it has gone *down* since 2019, by 1 percent.

And don't even get me started on race. When you segment out race as a factor, and break those percentages down by racial representation, you see that only roughly 22 percent of those characters are Black. And though that might seem like a lot, considering it's the largest minority demographic of LGBTQ representation, we still have a long way to go.

The numbers now seem better, and that makes me glad. But back *in my day*, we had barely 2 percent representation. And that 2 percent? Usually consisted of characters who were ashamed of being gay, suffering from AIDS, living in silence. The representation was there, but it wasn't great representation. It didn't make you proud to be gay.

So now, I find myself oftentimes, when watching shows, latching on to characters who help me hone and iron out the version of myself I want to be. Entertainment, from TV to movies, has always been a big source of safety for me. I wonder how different I'd be if I'd had these characters when I was seventeen. I wonder what person I'd have become. I don't know, but I do know these three characters have helped me get through some of the hardest of times, and more importantly, helped me define and create who I am today.

Ambrose, *Chilling Adventures of Sabrina*

Here's the thing. If I had to think of one character that described me more than any other character, it would be Ambrose from *Chilling Adventures of Sabrina*.

We all have those characters, right? The ones we identify with more than we probably should and who define everything about our personalities for as long as we can remember? Ambrose is that character for me. Sassy, confident, magical, and someone who is trying to atone for their sins? Count me in.

What I love most about Ambrose from *Chilling Adventures of Sabrina* is his unapologetic sense of self. There's no part in the show where I personally feel like his sexuality becomes such a focus that the character is lost. There isn't a point where I'm like, *Oh, the only thing of value Ambrose adds is his queer rep.* Yes, his being openly queer—specifically bisexual—is important, but it isn't the only thing about him that is important. Too often we see characters who are one-dimensional, where their queerness is the only thing people know about them or the only thing the directors feel like focusing on. Like, *Wow, yes, this character has the coolest magic ever, but they sleep with guys, so let's focus on that!*

Ambrose is a wizard, first and foremost. And he's a wizard with a pretty impressive history. We know, from the little bit the show gives us, that he was involved with some pretty messed-up stuff in the past, involving magic wars and terrorism—keeping it spoiler free for you all. This is a really interesting character, and it's a character that just happened to belong to the Rainbow Mafia. And even though Ambrose is bisexual, and not strictly gay, it's not often that we see Black characters who are so well defined, and so much more than their sexuality.

Ambrose is a complicated character, point-blank, who believes in helping Sabrina and his newfound family, the Spellmans. He falls in love with a woman but also has a sexual relationship with a man. He's witty, sarcastic, charming, intelligent, and powerful, and most important, he feels like a role model to me.

It's hard to exist in this world, as a fiction author, as someone who absorbs fantastical entertainment, without bringing up *Harry Potter*. Now, we're not going to give J. K. Rowling more space than she deserves, but as someone who grew up reading *Harry Potter*, I remember how it felt to want to be a wizard in the world she created. Wanting to belong and to go on those adventures.

But if you're someone who read the books, you know there are hardly any people of color in the stories. And when they do exist, they exist as caricatures of their race or are just thrown in there to check some weird box that she thought she needed to check. I never grew up, like so many girlfriends of mine, feeling like, *Oh I'm such a Hermione.* Or, *I'm a redhead so I'm totally a Ron.*

Ambrose to me was, as a Black queer man, the character that I could imprint myself on. I like to think I'm a pretty sarcastic person, to the point of almost being sardonic, but I also think that I believe in loyalty, in the power of family, in the power of friendships. I instantly latched on to this character because everything about him related to me and what I care about and what I consider a value. It helped me understand what it meant to actually see myself on the page when it had been so long since I felt like I had seen myself. If I'm being honest, I don't think I actually ever really saw myself until I saw Ambrose. I think there are many Black characters in different types of literature and other entertainment that are queer, but not enough to actually identify with me and fit beyond the checkboxes.

As I mentioned earlier, queer characters, and queer characters of color, are not something that just appeared in the past five years. But they've always been characters who seem like they are only there to teach lessons and warnings rather than fully thought-out characters. I don't know if this is on purpose, but I do know growing up seeing mostly characters who only existed to teach about how *having sex is bad*, or *how your family will never love you because you're Black and queer,* or a wealth of other lessons, really screwed up my sense of self for a long time. It made me think that I only exist in this world to either support or be somebody's lesson. To "atone for my sins" in some twisted way, or to actually be a Magical Queer Negro and help teach someone else, who was the main character of the story, how to grow.

As such, being in a millennial group around TV and movies, being a queer kid who was fairly lonely in high school and who spent a lot of time on the internet, this lesson led to my making some pretty bad choices. Now, I'm not gonna say that the choices weren't my own, and that TV and movies are the sole reason behind them, but when you grow up only seeing a certain version of yourself on the screen and you only see a certain type of ending, you end up actually internalizing that ending and thinking of it as the ending you deserve.

It's why the single-story narrative is such a dangerous thing. It's why to me, Ambrose was such an important and vital character.

Oliver Grayson, *The Bold Type*

What's one type of character that comes to mind when you think of queer characters on TV? I think there are three specific archetypes:

- The sidekick to the female main character.
- The fashion-obsessed, fairly shallow minor character who's only there to create quippy lines.
- And then we have the antagonist whose gayness is in some part connected to why they are evil.

These are the characters a lot of gay people grew up with. And then there's kind of the fourth archetype I don't really mention here, which is the character who's only gay because we were told they're gay from the outsider's point of view. I like to think of it as *The Rainbow Shattering of the Fourth Wall*.

This Rainbow Shattering of the Fourth Wall is more common than people like to think. About a month before this was written, I saw on Instagram a photo of four different announcements from Disney about how they were casting an LGBT character for the first time. Now, if you saw these in isolation and you weren't well read into media, you might think this was a huge accomplishment. But when you look carefully, you start to see that each one of these characters doesn't really matter for the movie. They don't really move the plot, and if you removed them, the movies would be the same.

Oliver Grayson is none of those things. In *The Bold Type*, Oliver Grayson is the head of a fashion department. He teaches our main characters about what it means to have power inside a system and organization that isn't going to love you back. He teaches one of the main characters how to be confident and take up space while at the same time how to learn and be gracious. Oliver to me doesn't fall under the Magical Negro there to help because he's more than just there to teach our character about the world she resides in and to help her grow.

When watching *The Bold Type*, I found a lot of power in Oliver as a character. For one, he has a husband, which isn't a common thing to see in TV among gay characters, especially Black gay characters, so I found him to be confident and competent without overstepping those boundaries. Oliver wasn't a character who was simply there to be bitchy just to be bitchy. He was there because he worked hard to get where he was, and he wasn't going to let anyone take that from him. Oftentimes Black characters, and Black people, are told they have to be twice as good if they want to succeed on the same level as their white counterparts. But what we don't often see, especially in cinema, is that you don't have to compromise yourself to get that success. Oliver personified this in a way that really taught me that as a Black and gay man, someone who exists in double minorities, it is possible to succeed and to not suffer along the way.

Oliver also personified something that I hadn't seen in cinema or in myself in a while. He personified a person who is willing to take up space. As a fashion director, Oliver was a character who had to fight tooth and nail to get where he was. I think we see this trope often in female characters, especially in female characters of color, but with gay characters, it's not really the same. It's hard for me to count on more than one hand, and even on that single hand probably on half as many fingers, the number of gay characters who have real positions of power. Oliver teaches our main character(s) how to navigate a system that is set up for her to fail. I think I learned a lot from Oliver because I identify with this. He's a queer Black man trying to navigate academia and then trying to navigate nonprofit and then trying to navigate corporate. Oliver taught me how to make space for myself, to realize how to shrink myself and to wiggle my way through cracks—and how not to compromise on my own self-worth.

These intersections aren't easy, and many people don't find

out how to navigate them for years. But I do attest a lot of my success, and my own skills as a leader and a worker, to Oliver Grayson as a character.

Pray Tell, *Pose*

I knew when I set out to write this essay that I wanted to focus on three Black men who changed the way I view myself as a person. Initially, I did a search for Black queer characters in cinema, and most of the lists came up with the same five to ten people. I did my best to try to remember the Black queer characters I had seen on TV growing up and try to establish if they had any lasting effect on me as a person and my growth as an individual.

If you knew me before you saw the name of this essay, you know that I am a young adult author. But I also write rom-coms, with the focus of putting Black and queer characters in the forefront and giving them happy endings. I wanted to focus on creating characters who have happy endings and who personify what it means to be Black and what it means to be queer in a positive light. I think, too often, Black characters—men and women, gay or straight, are used as a teachable moment for white readers and white consumers of media.

But I think there's a way to make accurate portrayals of stories of queer men of color, and dive into the dark underbelly of queer history, without simply making teachable moments out of tragedies. And when I was putting this list together, I wanted to focus on that. To find a character who to me was realistic and authentic and explored a side of queer history that's often not truly discussed in an authentic and respectful way, but also focused on the bad, and the good, in a respectful manner. When I narrowed my characters down, only one came to mind.

Billy Porter came to fame thanks to *Pose* and changed the world by being a groundbreaking, trendsetting icon. His portrayal of Pray Tell, the emcee of the balls where a large portion of *Pose* is set, is colorful. His portrayal of being a gay man in the '80s and '90s with HIV/AIDS is real, and the way he shows nuanced and informed points of view of the LGBTQ community, especially of the Black LGBTQ community, is important. Billy Porter lived through this harrowing time in history. He grew up as a gay Black man during this time in history, so what we see is realer than we could ever imagine.

But, for me, it's more than just a great character. Pray Tell is the personification of something bigger within the community. In the LGBTQ community, we kind of fall between being masculine and being feminine, at least that's how those outside the community view us. That binary idea of masculine and feminine, or its sister category, top and bottom, is really just a way to uphold the binary and help make straight people understand what it means to be gay, in an easily digestible way. We don't have enough time in this essay to really go into all the nuance of that. But I think most people would say that Billy Porter's character is more feminine than he is masculine.

There're a lot of people within the community and outside the community who look down on being feminine. Who view people as less than if they are more feminine. I don't know where I fall on that spectrum, and even as a thirty-year-old man, I'm not really sure if I'm comfortable using those definitions. I like things that some people would consider girly and I like things that some people would describe as being masculine. For a long time, I thought that having more feminine tendencies made me less than as a man and less than as a gay man. I thought it pigeonholed me into a very specific type of group, especially as a Black man, and limited who I could find as a lover in the spaces inside the LGBTQ community I could run in.

Which is why I think Pray Tell, to me, was such an awesome and important character. He pushes the norms by being somebody who conventional society might consider more feminine, but he's also someone who can kick your ass if he needs to. Pray Tell is flawed because he makes a lot of mistakes in the show that by today's conventions would be considered complete and total faux pas. He's selfish, quick to judge, power hungry, stubborn, and suffers from tunnel vision. But he learns, and more importantly, he makes most of his decisions because he believes in his family and the power of it.

I think that's an important lesson people often overlook: the value of family, both biological and found. Many people within the LGBTQ rainbow struggle with finding their "family" because many of us, for one reason or another, have lost our biological family. It's important we have cinema and literature that reinforces that our found family is just as important as a biological one. And as a whole, I think *Pose* teaches this lesson well and Pray Tell personifies what it means to be a member of a family, to be accepted for your flaws, and to accept others for theirs. That's important. That's a lesson we could use more of.

BEING QUEER IS hard. Navigating the world as one minority is a difficult thing—but as a double minority? Even harder. There're a lot of people trying to box you into a specific category and trying to help you decide who you are. Growing up and trying to understand what it meant to be Black and what it meant to be queer, even as an adult, has never been the easiest thing. I jokingly say it's like my third or fourth job. There definitely was a time in my life when I thought I could only be Black, or that I could only be queer.

But like what often happens with age, you learn more about yourself and learn more about the world around you. I am who I am as a person, still evolving, still changing, still growing, because of my family, because of my friends, because of what I consume. Sometimes I wonder how different I would be if I had been born thirty or forty years in the past. What type of person would I be if I hadn't had the assistance of some of the characters who were my safe havens—my educators, my teachers, and my friends as they grow older. What we absorb as entertainment has a direct effect upon who we are as people. That's why it's so important that we have characters, especially marginalized ones, that are authentic.

Authentic doesn't mean sugarcoating, where it only shows the good, and it most certainly doesn't mean traumatizing to only show the bad. There is space in our cinema for both. And often-times characters can—and should—personify both the good and the bad because that reflects the real world. Content creators have a responsibility, even if they don't want to admit it, to create characters that in some way, especially for content that targets teens, help them understand this complicated experience. Their life—known as being a teenager. Many studies have shown that the teenage years are the most important years for development. So why don't we try to help guide them through these compli-cated times as much as possible?

Growth also doesn't stop when we turn twenty. In fact, I'd argue that I grew more in my twenties than I did in my teens. Not because life was harder or more fruitful but because I knew more about myself and who I wanted to be in my twenties than in my teens. I'm glad I had these characters to help me grow, and as an author, I hope to create characters that'll help another twentysomething or teen grow, too.

That's why I do what I do. I think if you had asked me a month, or even a year ago, about why I write queer Black characters in love stories, in thrillers, in quiet adventures, I would have told you because it feels right. But I wouldn't exactly know why. This is why. I write these stories because Black queer characters have helped teach me things about myself and still do to this day. I write and create these characters, not only in the hope of making that 9 percent larger, but also in the hope of making a character who will help change another teen or young adult's life. Some-one whom they can imprint on and use as a blueprint for their personality. Someone they can use as a catalyst to help get them through a rough patch of their life. As a writer, as a member of the global community, and as someone who wants to make their mark, there is no bigger joy.

But, right now, I'm just going to focus on marathoning my next TV show.

In Search of the Black Historical Hottie Hero

The Sad Situation of the Black Hero in Historical Romance

PIPER HUGULEY

The commercial first ran during the Super Bowl in 2021. Allstate. A successful, handsome young Black man living the American dream. Nice car, open road, driving fast, singing the Pet Shop Boys song "Opportunities"—all about making money. It's a Black Lives Matter plus capitalist love connection in the making. Black folks are being represented. We have our share of the pie—finally. What could be wrong?

Nothing.

Until the hood ornament of the car, an inanimate object, opens her metallic mouth and joins in the singing with him, singing: "You've got the brawn, I've got the brains. Let's make lots of money!"

Ummm excuse me? Just what is Miss Hood Ornament trying to say? That's the moment the commercial turns sour for me.

It's too much to take in a 2021 moment—not when there's George Floyd with a knee on his neck, not when the NFL admits "race-norming" to deny Black men payment for their head injuries.

I can't sing along to the '80s tune anymore. It's just one more reminder that Black men have a long, long way to go to be considered heroic in the US of A.

Others will point to progress. What of the duke in *Bridgerton*? Everyone just about had a hissy fit because he wouldn't be returning for season two. They don't even care about his lady love. They just want the duke.

And we've had a Black president—a handsome one. Someone whose every word, even his book recommendation lists, carries a lot of weight.

Michael B. Jordan, Denzel Washington, and Will Smith are powerful movie stars and producers. Everyone cried when Chadwick Boseman died. Black men are a part of heroism, aren't they?

Not really. The stereotypes that have bedeviled Black men are still a large part of our twenty-first-century life and form a large reason for why romance readers don't accept Black men as heroes in historical romance.

MY JOURNEY IN thinking through this started out in 2010. I had been on a writing break and was getting back into the swing of writing after ten years of being away. This time, I reinvented myself as a historical romance person, in large part due to my belief that the audience that loved and appreciated Ms. Beverly Jenkins, queen of the Black historical romance, might be in need of more historical romance stories to read. I could try appealing to them in a slightly different way.

While Ms. Bev went super hot with the sexy times in her landmark historical romances like *Indigo* and *Night Song*, I would close the door in my Black Southern romances. I would focus on the faith journey of my characters and show what made those characters strong and powerful, and capable of maintaining happy inner lives that allowed them to deal with and overcome dehumanization in the larger society. To me, in 2010, too many Black folks seemed to have forgotten that and how the ancestors endured their difficulties. I thought, if I added my voice to the Black historical romance choir, people could see that we had, indeed, come a long way and could weather any storms that a phenomenon such as the Tea Party might bring to us.

So, I determined that I would write historical romances showing Black love, and I would tell stories that were foregrounded in the reality of Black life in their time period. I would provide focus on the Black hero who was willing to be courtly and chivalrous to win the love of the Black heroine, in rather short order—of course. There's only so long that young people can go without wanting to come together for the sexy times. I felt I could write to that, and leave the door closed, since my skills did not extend to writing scenes that highlighted the slots and tabs of lovemaking.

The central question for my first series was: What would a Black Prince Charming look like in 1915 Georgia? Not a duke, certainly. Instead, it would be someone who had a lot of education, much more than the average Black Southern man, who typically had eight years or less of schooling. A doctor. And because colorism was so prevalent at this time period, a very light-skinned doctor—someone who would have had no trouble passing over the color line to get his education, à la James Weldon Johnson's *The Autobiography of an Ex-Colored Man*.

However, he couldn't be a Prince Charming in my book if he opted to stay on the white side, as the hero of Johnson's story did. No. The heroic thing would be to learn that there were costs to passing for white, like the loss of his soul. Who would be the better teacher for such a story than a fiery, equally light-skinned heroine who had been living as a Negro for years and recognized his falsity, and wanted to show him the light of embracing his Blackness? She would show him the best side of being real and true, as a way to help their people to a better way of life.

So, Adam Morson, the hero of *A Virtuous Ruby*, was born. Adam, a Black man who had been passing for white for years, would learn all the ins and outs of Blackness that he had been avoiding. He becomes heroic when he sees and appreciates all the parts of his identity. Then, rather than do the things that his distant father wanted him to do, rather than seek his approval, he does the heroic thing by protecting the woman and child he loves and gets them out of harm's way. Adam takes what is most valuable—his new family, his labor, his ideas, his intelligence—and leaves, not wanting to benefit a town that sought to quell his freedom to be a Black man. However, readers interpreted Adam's actions in a Western way: accusing him of running away.

An alpha male hero, the standard in historical romance, would not run away from a hard time, but that's not looking through the lens of how a Black man in 1915 would see the situation.

Asa Caldwell, the World War I veteran hero of *A Most Precious Pearl*, was my next attempt at my type of Black hero. Due to a dustup with a racist sergeant in the military, Asa lost his lower left leg. When he arrives in Winslow, Georgia, in 1919, he is still dealing with the PTSD aspects of the war because he's reminded that he must fight another war in the United States as a reporter on the front lines of racial injustice in the South. A South that's on the verge of the Red Summer of 1919. He's reluctant to go south to report on potential lynching crimes, but he cannot help becoming enmeshed in the struggles of the community. Ultimately, he returns home to Pittsburgh, but insists that the heroine he has fallen for, Margaret Bledsoe, accompany him there. In the climax scene of the story, Asa gets Margaret to understand that by leaving, she benefits herself. She will no longer allow her employer at the mill to have access to her innovations, her creativity, and her management capabilities. In this persuasion, as well as his admiration of Margaret, he is a hero—one worthy of Margaret's love and the respect of the Black community he writes reports on lynching for. Asa was not running away from difficulty.

Jay Evans, in *A Treasure of Gold*, is representative of a Black man who, because of racism, has to resort to illegal activity in order to make a better standard of living for his wife and daughter. He's not a criminal. His skill with mathematics in some other place, in a body of another race, might have meant that he would have become a world-renowned mathematician, or a professor in a flagship university. But that prized skill in a Black man in 1923 Pittsburgh can only be used in the policy numbers racket with Jay as the head of the racket. His heroics involve giving up the illegality of the game when he recognizes that he is putting the woman and child he loves in danger. He also realizes he can create opportunity for his community by establishing a bank. His willingness to think in a broader and more expansive way is at odds with an individualistic, self-centered mindset that a typical alpha hero might show. This, coupled with Jay's dalliance with criminal activity, also renders him as non-heroic.

For years, romance heroes were not permitted to come from the realms of sports or entertainment. However, Kimani Romance, which published contemporary romance featuring Black characters in the early 2010s, broke through this expectation early on, by featuring R&B singers and sports heroes in their romances. This set the stage for other authors in Romancelandia to establish subgenres that readers believed to be new—sports romance and music-industry-based romances that did not feature Black characters.

However, sports have always played an important role in Black life. So Champion Bates, my hero in *A Champion's Heart*, whom I set up as a fictitious precursor to Jack Johnson, was a boxer who paved the way for interracial fights, a convention of boxing that had been done away with after Jack Johnson lost the World Heavyweight title. In order to help the love of his life get her mini-orphanage to safety, he agrees to fight one more match, defying doctor's orders and risking his sight on her behalf. To make his actions more heroic, he has to earn money at the height of the Great Depression to secure their future. However, some readers were concerned that the heroine would be "stuck with" a blind man as her husband. There were also concerns that as a former boxer, Champion did not make enough money to be able to support a family. The money concern was a reminder to me that one of the expectations of romance is that the hero be able to make enough money to ensure that the happy couple will not want for anything. This is a crucial component to being a hero, and Champion's career choices were a concern.

Virgil Smithson, in my Home to Milford College series, represented one of the more difficult situations in constructing a hero. The first book in the series was set in 1866, and Virgil was formerly enslaved and illiterate. Romance doesn't feature heroes who are enslaved, because being held in enslavement means that the character doesn't have agency or freedom to choose—two things that are essential in a romance fiction character. However, Virgil manages to earn enough money with his blacksmithing business to buy himself free. He also wanted to buy his wife and child free, heroic enough, but being free means that he has to leave Georgia. He must send money back to the family who owns them. Unbeknownst to him, they sell his wife off to another owner who does not treat her well, and she dies. So when readers first meet Virgil, it's clear that he has trust issues before he can meet up with the woman who will be his new wife. In Milford, Georgia, he has to navigate an atmosphere that is hostile to his right to be free, even though the Civil War has come to an end.

One of the scenes that readers commented on was when Virgil took Northern-raised Amanda to the store. He tells her how to behave in the Southern way before they go, with her head down, no eye contact, and to let him do all the talking. She doesn't remember his instruction and, by behaving in a different way, puts their lives in jeopardy. He has to make her understand her new life in the South:

> Amanda found Virgil mucking out the horses' stalls. A thankless boring task to be sure, but one she knew was necessary to keep a horse's shoes in pristine condition.
>
> She folded her arms over herself to keep her emotions in check. "Missed you at the Saturday school."
>
> "Not going into that schoolhouse while other folk is there."
>
> "You don't think of it as an opportunity to set a good example?"
>
> "No. Take me longer than everyone else to learn. People see I ain't fit to be the mayor and run me out of the office."
>
> "Oh, Virgil. Why are you so hard on yourself?"
>
> "And who are you to be saying such things?"
>
> "I'm your wife, if you've forgotten."
>
> He turned to adjust a harness, then spoke. "No. Haven't forgotten. Can't forget."
>
> What did that mean? How sorry he was to be saddled with her for the rest of his life? Well, she was too. What about what she felt? "Fine then. We have to make the best of this situation."
>
> "Doing what I can."
>
> "As am I."
>
> He stopped his mucking. "Sometimes lessons aren't just in books."

"I'm fully aware of that."

"I'm your husband."

"I understand that as well." She rubbed her arms to warm herself.

"You need to trust me when I say do."

"Sometimes I feel . . ."

Virgil put down his pitchfork and stepped closer. He wore his informal clothes today and had been working hard. His manly scent of sweat and horses mixed together clouded her mind. He had a fine sheen of sweat on his face, and his eyebrows drew together in displeasure. He took her by the arm. "Sometimes it's about what's in here." He took her hand and placed it on his chest. "Right here. There's a feeling here says danger."

The hardness of his chest caused her hand to almost bounce off. She cleared her throat. "Of course. There's always conflict between the head and the heart."

"Then that's you and me. You the head. I'm the heart. Sometimes you got to trust the heart."

Oh my. The heart. The seat of all that was emotional and unsure. Hers was surely pounding up now. "I see."

"I wonder what you see up in that educated mind of yours. Everything don't work out as it do in books."

"Alpha heroes in romance don't behave in this way," I was told. Virgil's behavior, intended to protect the woman he loves, a key feature of alpha heroes, was seen as weak and unheroic. The expectations of alpha heroism ran up against real-life Black history. The two did not jibe.

A similar problem occurred in my novella *A Sweet Way to Freedom*, where the hero, Arlo Tucker, is an alcoholic who has two young children and has fathered another one on the way—all three out of wedlock in 1910 Winslow. The story involves Arlo's search for his purpose in the world, trying to protect his new love and family while dealing with his issues with the bottle, something that was difficult to do since he runs the local town juke joint. His walk away from alcohol involves the need to select a new profession, one that ensures that he make enough money. He seeks to reassure the heroine, the mother of his coming child, that he has plans for this new addition and their family:

"Missy, I grew up without a pappy and I don't want that for this child. I'm not as bad as you say. I'll do for this child."

"Long as it's a boy, right? Should I ask Kate and Addy's mothers about how and what you do? No. You might want to get on to the spool-winding room of the towel mill to see if there are any young girls who are interested. Only, everyone here in Winslow knows how you do. Including your nieces you seem to be so fond of . . ."

He shrugged, striking a funny pose. The last thing, nearly the very last thing he wanted was her hurt. That was the reason why he had to stay away from her. "Their mothers. I got to tell you about them. Then you can decide if you want anything to do with me."

Her smile disappeared and her bottom lip quivered. "Why wouldn't I? I need all the help I can get. I'm all alone in the world in this."

"That's not true."

He went to her and embraced her, awkwardly from the side, as if he didn't know how to hold her anymore. Missouri didn't move. Didn't turn her body to him, didn't respond in any way.

No use. Didn't she love him just the least little bit? But if she didn't want to listen to what he had to say . . . what could he do? All of his bad luck was hard to take in, even for himself.

Dropping his arms, he moved to the door, opened it, and stepped through into the steamy late May night, feeling as roasted as the beef in the stew.

There were times when freedom felt humid. Sticky wet, with a heaviness inside of him, just like the small, wet circles on Missouri Baxter's shirtwaist.

Arlo's struggles with alcohol were too realistic for some. Once again, he was considered less than heroic because of his rough and bumpy past. The term *pathetic* was applied in one review of the novella.

Interestingly enough, romance has had quite a history of dukes who have had problems with alcohol, opium, and drugs of all kind. There are an infinite number of historical romance heroes who have littered the English countryside (and it is usually England) with multitudes of illegitimate children. However, readers don't see these heroes as an issue or a problem. It's only when a Black man is engaged in a real struggle with alcohol and fights to find his way to redemption that these tropes are an issue.

And therein lies the problem with the full acceptance of the

Black historical hero into Romancelandia. These heroes have to combat reader expectations of the historical Black man. There is little room, apparently, for Black male heroes to be heroes in their own culture, in their own way. Having "enough" money isn't enough. There is too much historical baggage. There will always be a little metallic lady saying he doesn't have brains.

So, as a consequence, we don't have as many of them.

Readers will bring up other historical romance authors. What about Beverly Jenkins? Or Alyssa Cole? These wonderful authors have done wonderful things with the Black male historical heroes they have written. Their Black historical heroes exist, sure, better than historical heroes of other races or ethnicities, but overall, there are probably no more than fifty, compared to the thousands upon thousands of dukes who exist in historical romance.

Given this track record, the decline of the numbers of Black historical hottie heroes makes complete sense. We probably won't see many more of them in the future.

Interracial Romance and the Single Story

JESSICA P. PRYDE

I am a poster child for the romance industry's favorite interracial relationship.

I met the man who would eventually become my spouse on move-in day of my freshman year at a Private White Institution named for a slave owner. We knew each other for a couple of years before we fell into dating, and then proceeded to go All In and move across the country together a few times, getting married along the way. He is as white as white can be—a whole blue circle of white European on the genealogy report. He likes guitars, baseball, and Martin Scorsese movies. He's also an amazing partner who sends me animal videos and memes when I'm sad, feeds me when I forget, and acts as a buffer when the world is shit—which is more often than not, nowadays. And thanks to circumstance, happenstance, and a bit of human nature, here we are, and will continue to be.

Mine is a relationship, a Black woman married to a white man, that just a few years ago wasn't quite taboo but was definitely not always seen in entertainment media. When it was featured, it was probably the central conflict of the story, whether it was an episode of a television show or the basis of a whole book or movie. It was only in the past few years that we started to see interracial couples more—in commercials, as central narratives of television shows, as the main characters in romance novels, happy ending included. And very often, it is that very specific interracial relationship: Black woman, white man. Abishola and Bob. Uhura and Spock. Rainbow Johnson's parents. It's become one of the more prominently depicted relationships across media, even though a research study from 2017 stated that Black men were twice as likely to marry outside their race as Black women. In romance novels in particular, whether or not they've been written by Black authors, it is more likely that the average reader will see Black protagonists with white love interests in the mainstream, no matter the character's gender and sexual identity.

THANKS TO AN ever-burning need for books with happy endings, I have been gravitating toward romance for most of my life. (It's weird to say that, but I've got more years on the northern side of fifteen than the south.) In the earliest days, I didn't think romance books could have Black characters, or be written by Black authors. I'd found books like *The Color Purple* and *The Coldest Winter Ever*, books that are amazing works of literature, but not what I was looking for. I found some teen books in the library that I'll sadly never recall the titles or authors of twenty-five years later, but not romances like the ones I grabbed off the top shelf in the basement when my mother, grandmother, and aunt were done with them. Books by Jude Deveraux, Johanna Lindsey, and Janelle Taylor filled my tween years, long before I understood how harmful some of their common traits and tropes could be, including kidnapping and rape—without saying the words *kidnapping* and *rape*. Or some incredibly racist, Orientalist plots. The Westernized twin taking over the Caliphate and the harem, degrading his Eastern heritage the whole time. The Confederate soldier finding his true love cowboying out West after the war. The English nobleman lording over his serfdom, expectant to lord over his new wife, all the same.

In high school, I veered into more varied reading, though happy endings were still a must. After an AP Language paper on *Pride and Prejudice* steered me into a near decade-long detour into fan fiction for several different properties (more guaranteed happy endings, all for free), I spent a few more years focusing on young adult books for my job as a high school librarian. But that job's constant stressors required an outlet, and I landed firmly back in the romance camp, thanks in part to Beverly Jenkins's *Destiny's Surrender* and Farrah Rochon's New York Sabers, a football series initially published by Kimani, Harlequin's now-defunct Black romance line. While the majority of my reading still featured white protagonists, I always sought out more Black authors—bonus if they were queer (but that's another story for another day). A couple of years later, Alyssa Cole's *Let It Shine*—

a romance set during the American civil rights era featuring a young Black woman finding her voice and the boy, himself a child of Russian immigrants, who would join her on the Freedom Ride—would fall into my lap. From that point, white love interests were a more common feature as I continued to discover more romance by Black authors.

There are probably multiple reasons for this—some my own fault, others more the fault of publishing at large. While I had access to several different bookstores as a teenager and younger adult, some of which were more open to carrying romance than others, they didn't often carry books from Black lines like Arabesque, Kimani, and Dafina. Early on, I had been easily disappointed by books by Black authors that were better classified as "chick lit" or women's fiction—family or relationship dramas that didn't offer the same happy ending that my mother's pocket romances did. So I avoided those books and the ones on the shelves around them. Instead, I picked up books about people so far removed from my daily life, it wasn't even noticeable how breathtakingly white my reading was. And I didn't have that same online collection of go-to trusted folks that I could hear and learn from in regard to new books, like I do now. I mostly relied on friends and family to surface new reading for me, whether at home, school, or work in the summers. When I finally started picking books with visible Black people off the shelves of bookstores and libraries (and eventually, the iBooks and Kindle books stores), my most prominent options were often romances with interracial couples. On Amazon in particular, in the African American section of the romance page, I would try one or two of those clearly labeled but under-edited BWWM (Black Woman White Man) romances, hoping one might catch me enough to find a new author to follow. But I learned to scroll past the ones—heavily reliant upon a specific stock image collection—whose covers suggested the story was about less-well-off Black women finding wealthy white partners to step up in life, often with at least one child in the mix. White love interests could be anything from professional athletes to doctors to a member of that unspecified and incongruous group of "billionaires," while the Black women often worked in the service industry or some other underappreciated career path. Many of the familiar tropes abound—one-night stand, marriage of convenience, single parent and caretaker, etc. And many of them were obviously created by the same person or group of people (often called a mill), and yet they often dominated that section of romance. These books obviously have their audience, but I was looking for something . . . else.

I'm not sure what I was expecting of that "else," but I stumbled into the pockets of online media that led me toward a few authors who were either self-publishing or working with smaller presses and imprints. Even as recently as five years ago, marketing opportunities for self-published authors were fewer and farther between, and there were very specific Black Books that the Big Five and Big Independent publishers would promote. Whether it was Harlequin, Kensington, or Avon, there were only a few books I'd hear about in the common spheres, whether it was via print marketing, social media, press releases, or direct email. (And sometimes, those were the only books by Black authors they were publishing anyway, if one were to look at the seasonal release catalogs.) As the publishing lines that had been developed strictly to produce content featuring Black characters continued to fade away—first Arabesque, then Kimani—characters of color were pushed to digital-first imprints like Carina Press and Avon Impulse. Big names like Brenda Jackson, who published her first novel in 1995 and has since published over 100 romance novels, cut through some of the noise, but marketing dollars and publicist hours were spent elsewhere for a very long time. The ones that did get a push or two always seemed to be books by Black authors featuring at least one white character. The rest, we were just expected to find by osmosis, or using our powers as Sage Magical Negroes. Publishers can say, "at least they were published," but their lower sales numbers (thanks in part to lack of marketing) more than likely contributed to their culling, until those same familiar names were once again the only ones we were seeing.

IN A CONVERSATION with Black romance author (and *Black Love Matters* contributor) Christina C. Jones, she pointed out the "constant erasure of romantic relationships between Black lovers." That particular wording set something afire in me. This is an issue in all media, among book publishers and filmmakers alike—whether it's romance novels, television series, movies, or any of the slew of other forms of media that we regularly take in. Case in point: over the 2020 football season, I noticed a common family unit, primarily in car commercials but also in other kinds of advertisements: Black woman, white man, racially ambiguous children. Over and over. Driving up into the mountains; pulling up to a drive-in at a diner; enjoying a meal together. It wasn't always the same family, or even the same car company. But it was definitely a trend. On television and at the movies, romantic plots designed for "broader audiences" often present a strong, work-oriented Black woman and the white man she falls for, whether in the span of ninety minutes or several seasons. *The Incredible Jessica James*, which I enjoy for Jessica Williams's delightful portrayal and other reasons funny only to me, is a prime example of that same kind of strong Black woman who finds herself in a Happy For Now (HFN) situation with a Perfectly Nice White Guy. Shonda's Thursday nights, too, have been heavy with them for years, and other networks working to match her appeal followed suit. And in the heavily evident case of Shondaland, the show's writers would do anything in their power to make it nearly impossible for the Strong Black Woman and her white lover to be together, and definitely not happily or easily. This can regularly include the death or other permanent removal of the white love interest—because Black women can't keep nice things. Perhaps, on television drama, nobody can keep nice things—but it feels incredibly visceral when it happens so regularly to a demographic who is so irregularly seen across networks.

No matter what it may sound like, I don't seek to condemn these relationships in media. I don't seek to condemn the creators of the media that feature successful Black/white interracial relationships more than successful Black relationships. I love seeing these stories well presented just as I do any other romantic story, because romance is my air. But it is an inescapable fact that romantic media seems more likely to be produced by major companies and consumed by the greater white population if it features half of a Black couple instead of a whole one. The biggest example from 2020 and 2021 was definitely *Bridgerton*, which was built from the blocks of a very white historical romance series. But the most talked-about character is the Duke of Hastings, portrayed by the completely beautiful, very much Black Regé-Jean Page. In less than a month, it became Netflix's most popular series ever. This one was particularly exemplary of the Black/white relationship, because for once the Black man was the central character. But since the Bridgertons are the central characters of that universe, they must still be white, while love interests of any gender, who are not part of the core cast, might come and go by season.

And America's ongoing favorite real-life love story, Harry and Meghan, is that same relationship played out for them in real life.

There are exceptions; there are always exceptions. Whether it's a new Kenya Barris series in the Black-ish universe or the regularly scheduled "discovery" of Beverly Jenkins among mainstream romance audiences, Black lovers do appear in pockets for the mainstream to discover. But so many of those exceptions only appear when we shift to production companies whose mission is to center them. Cable networks like OWN and BET. Kensington's Dafina line, streaming companies that focus on Black content. And while love is love and people will continue to fall in love with who they will (like I did), there is something to be said for the distressing default to interracial that we see in the mainstream.

As a Black woman who has grown up in a white supremacist society, I get it. The interracial couple in popular media—especially film—is a misguided effort to make Black people more palatable to white audiences. Black men are still considered too intimidating to white women to consider them love interests to people of any race; so for the sake of still allowing female audiences to self-insert, they can take the place of the Black woman main character and still get their white dream man. Or at least, this is what it feels like. Similarly, in romance novels, if the Black female protagonist has a white love interest, it's much more relatable than a Black couple, even if they live similar lives to the reader. Filmmakers, showrunners, and publishers haven't outright said this in as many words, but we can see the plot. We've seen white women say it with their whole chests on social media.

"I just can't relate to these characters, because we don't share the same life experience."

"The language they use is very off-putting for me."

"This story [featuring well-off Black people] didn't feel like it would be historically accurate."

I'll be the first to say some of my favorite romantic stories feature interracial couples, whether starring a Black and white couple or a couple featuring a Black person paired with a non-Black person of color. *Guess Who*, as ridiculous as it is, has a special place in my heart. *Romeo Must Die* has some serious problems but a killer soundtrack. *The Incredible Jessica James*, which I mentioned before, is . . . well, incredible. *The Lovebirds* is so funny it's embarrassing. And *Juanita* is one of the best pieces of film literature I've ever seen, especially considering the older, darker-skinned woman at its center. While not always helmed by Black creators, these films still ensure that their Black protagonists aren't just white characters dyed a darker brown with a few "cultural markers" thrown in for spice. (See Thandiwe Newton's character in *Mission Impossible 2* or Simone Payton from Penny Reid's *Dr. Strange Beard*—and many other Black female love interests written with good intentions by white romance authors.) These creators wrote their characters as complete people with insider knowledge about how life works for Black people when interacting with majority culture. Anytime a character deals with a microaggression, or wraps their hair at night, or expertly code-switches from interaction to interaction—or even something as simple as an expertly placed ribbing at a dance party—it feels more like a Black person than a caricature of one.

Some of my favorite contemporary Black romance authors have a history of pairing Black protagonists with love interests of other races and backgrounds. Rebekah Weatherspoon, Alyssa Cole, Talia Hibbert, and a number of others give romance readers Black characters that are fully formed and comfortable in their Blackness, but still—because of circumstance, happenstance, and a bit of human nature—find their romantic futures with non-Black characters, often white. The happiness of one (or two) Black people in the midst of a great romantic relationship is still valid and vital, and there are Black creators, whether they are working under the canopy of a bigger white awning or their own, who know how to make it work.

These authors aren't the only romance writers offering up interracial romance to the mainstream, either. It's not uncommon to pick up a series by a white or other non-Black author who's found an easy way to make their writing "more diverse" by offering a Black love interest to a member of the predominantly white group of men around whom their ongoing series centers. Whether brothers or brothers in arms, these men fall one by one for the woman they're meant to be with, and somewhere down the line, an editor suggested they might want to mix it up. And so more white men could remain the love interest for the self-insert reader while the Black romantic lead was left with few markers of actually being Black.

If these stories, whether in print or on-screen, are the only ones that mainstream consumers can name when asked about Black love stories, then they are not getting the full spectrum of Black love. And if that is the one story they know, some of these concepts—the idea that Black love is dead, that Black men don't have emotions, and that Black women are made to fix white men, or to act as conduits for them fixing themselves—will perpetuate in both mainstream media and real life.

And that's when people consume any media with central Black characters at all.

The problem when these relationships appear prominently in the eyes of people looking to diversify their own reading, or to even come to the fold because they feel they finally see representation, either for the first time or after a long drought, is that the books and media being pushed their way predominantly center Black women and white men. Black women, the majority of Black romance readers, were seeing themselves represented in books and films made by Black creators. It felt like progress. But what does it mean that there are still so few Black men being represented in mainstream romance and romantic arcs? When you scroll through streaming platforms, you see more Black men in action leads with mediocre romantic plots, if they have any. For those Black men we do see in relationships, very often they have already been firmly established; they're the couple who are already married, might even already have kids. We don't get to travel with them on their romantic journey. With a small number of exceptions, prominent cis male Black authors and other Black writers who were assigned male at birth aren't known for publishing happy love stories for adults—though maybe they're writing them and can't sell them to mainstream publishers whose only idea of Blackness, particularly when centering Assigned Male at Birth (AMAB) people, is trauma.

There will continue to be some implicit bias and internalized racism that contributes to this ongoing lack. We might be able to see Black men as superheroes and doctors and firefighters and teachers and roommates. But the ones who don't already come into the world with an established relationship aren't always able to find their One True Partner, and when they do, they're rarely white—*Bridgerton* being the obvious exception. If this feels like a double standard, with the prominence of the Black/white pairing with the genders switched, it is. But it lends more credence to the idea that Black love is less popular in mainstream media in part because of the need to make that relationship less intimidating to the average white reader or viewer.

IN AN ARTICLE from the *New York Times* from May 2020, Salamishah Tillet writes about the ongoing balance of interracial love and power. "[Control] and coercion," she says, "are inescapable in interracial relationships." For Black people in the United States and other places that have a history of colonization and chattel slavery, there has always been a concern of offset power dynamics in relationships between Black women and white men (or white women or white gender-nonconforming people, to a lesser extent). Taught the story of Thomas Jefferson and Sally Hemings at a young age, we were presented with the idea that some enslavers could love their enslaved captives. That no social construct could get in the way of True Love. This is a false narrative: no captive, especially a fifteen-year-old enslaved girl, can truly consent to a sexual relationship with their captor. And whether there was affection involved, the complications of their roles (and, you know, the fact that good old TJ didn't particularly believe that Black people were people, let alone equals) would not have allowed for a true romantic partnership. Two hundred years later, there are still complications and power balances in romantic relationships featuring a white person of any gender and a Black person, built from the same source. But Tillet concludes her article with the hopeful observation—in media, at least—of "a happily ever after in which the male partner acknowledges and begins to unravel his own racial privilege, not just out of love, but because it is the right thing to do."

While this hasn't always been the case in interracial romance stories, even written by Black authors, we can see it seeded in newer media. The white partners of Black romantic heroines (and some queer protagonists of all genders) have begun to meet their partners right where they are. They, like the partners in Tillet's hopeful future, know their own privilege and the setbacks their Black partners must face in order to live anything close to a worthwhile existence. They stand beside their partner when they need it, or behind them for the battles that need to be fought on their own. The difference in race isn't the central conflict now like it might have been in the 1990s with Sandra Kitt's *The Color of Love* or in the 2000s with *Something New*, starring Sanaa Lathan and Eyebrows Baker. Now, that difference might contribute to an understanding (or lack thereof), but the constant microaggressions that Black people of all genders have to deal with when in a romantic relationship with someone of any other race are somewhat removed, for the most part. In order to contribute to the element of escapist fantasy we might be looking for, especially as Black readers, it might be shown as light ribbing from friends or family of the Black protagonist, instead of seedy inferences or outright insult from someone else. Even then, if the Black protagonist's white allies are called to the table for a race-related or cultural misapprehension, time might be taken to approach it without forcing that Black main character to be a Magical Negro whose only purpose is to guide that white person to understanding themselves, their error, and the world. Missteps are made, pointed out, apologized for, and corrected. The story moves on. At least, if this story is the one that's going to be repeatedly told, we can have this modeling of an ideal way to live it.

MY YOUTH WAS filled with the promise of Black love on television and at the movies. I had less exposure to books, personally, but know they were there. Regardless of my crushes on Jonathan Taylor Thomas and the Backstreet Boys, I still had countless examples of Black relationships that weren't representative of my three-generation matriarchal household growing up, but were clear indications of what life could potentially be for me in the future. But today, media's efforts to go "post racial" and the desegregation of media have led to fewer prominent examples of Black relationships of all kinds—and only a few people in control of those narratives. That kind of siloing has led to a much smaller collection of perspectives and types of storytelling. In romance novels, we are seeing a much larger collection of those classic Black love stories from new and veteran authors—and those who are using the popularity they gained from writing interracial romances to tell more Black stories. Whether it's Jasmine Guillory, Alyssa Cole, or Vanessa Riley, the audiences they've built have (mostly) happily shifted with them from one kind of story to the other, and publishers have reluctantly realized they don't have to silo their authors into one kind of storytelling either.

Yes, romance writers. Use that system.

Of course, it's a double-edged sword—if Black characters are always paired with other Black characters, especially in ongoing television or film series, then it feels like they're being segregated. But if no Black characters are paired together? That feels pretty bad, too. It would be nice if we had a balance of the two, but we're often jerked in either direction, forced to choose what camp we're in.

In a soapy television series where there is plenty of racial diversity, a story arc presents itself in which a regular Black woman is paired with a recurring white male colleague. There are serious power issues, but they make it work. When the inevitable happens and they're torn apart by circumstances, that Black woman is next paired with a Black man, and there's potential chemistry with another. Neither works out. In another show, an interracial couple bring a third into their relationship. He is white, and she's multiracial (one Black parent, one Indigenous). As the show goes on, the white man and the white woman who has become part of the trio grow closer, pushing their darker partner out. Eventually, she flirts with a relationship with another non-white person. (We'll never know what happens with them because the show was canceled.) Even in something with as broad a cast as *Doctor Who*, we discover during a special that Martha and Mickey—Black companions to different Doctors, both of whom previously had partners of different races—are now together. To some, these kinds of relationship evolutions might feel like a weird form of bait and switch. We might want more Black couples in our media, but not at the expense of the relationships those people were already in. Just give us more. Give us balance.

———————

ROMANCE PUBLISHING IS definitely coming to their senses when it comes to telling more stories about Black characters in the mainstream; the joy over Harlequin Desire covers as each one featuring a Black couple is revealed is clear. But while the awareness of Black romance continues to grow, what does that actual readership look like? The individual number of Goodreads ratings for many of these titles is worlds below those for more popular Black writers publishing splashy interracial romance. But we can continue to wonder, who is picking up Black romance books in Walmart, or at the library, and not mentioning them to anyone else at all? While Harlequin's familiar name might allow them to edge into bigger markets, they lead the way for others to be able to sell and heavily promote Black authors who are writing the story that is more familiar to them—the insular love that came from growing up with specific role models, specific desires, in Black communities that allowed for the exchange that would lead to Black love. It's not just for Twitter, but for these readers, that the expansion beyond that single, interracial romance story that is so prominent in marketing and media is so important.

Even as a Black woman married to a white man who has to work on his own racial privilege every day, there's still nothing like seeing love between two (or more) Black people. These are the relationships my family built, my friends, my neighbors. I love to experience all kinds of love stories, between all kinds of people, but that serotonin hit when I see two Black people loving and supporting each other, sharing life experiences, goals, and desires—that's the stuff. And so I work every day to balance that appreciation. Because I know that the representation of interracial lovers isn't going anywhere. Not while the biggest producers of print and film media in Western society, on both sides of the Atlantic and around the world, still default to interracial as the more palatable option.

Romance Has Broken My Dichotomous Key

SARAH HANNAH GÓMEZ

There is no shortage of "there are two kinds of people in the world" memes. My personal favorite is "There are three kinds of Pilates teachers in the world: those who can count, and those who can't."

You see, it's a joke because when we say "Eight more," you may get as few as four and as many as fourteen more reps, and also because one of the foundational exercises in the discipline is called The Hundred, and you'll do anywhere from 80 to 120 reps because we're not actually counting, no matter what we tell you. A Nobel Prize–winning mathematician could teach Pilates in their spare time and they would not be able to keep count of reps in The Hundred. But now that I've had to explain the joke, and we're not even in a Pilates studio together, it's not funny.

Pilates is just my side job, however. What I have spent most of my adult life doing is[1] hanging out in academia. Humanities academia, to be exact. As a literature-focused scholar, I'm most concerned with dichotomies in approaches to reading. Binaries are useful. They're also a lie, or at the very least an incomplete story.

Two of my favorite dichotomies come from Roland Barthes and Louise Rosenblatt. Barthes, whom you should not bother reading because he is a total drag, used his to define impacts reading can have on a person; Rosenblatt, who is actually rather interesting and worth reading if you like layperson-friendly critical theory, used hers to describe different motivations for reading.

Roughly, Barthes's binary goes like this: there are two ways to enjoy a novel, jouissance and plaisir. You must say them with a French accent or it's no fun. *Plaisir* literally translates to "pleasure," which you may have guessed, and conveniently enough the simplest way to describe it is pleasure reading. You open a book, you get transported, all of a sudden, it's been six hours and your butt has fallen asleep, but you feel immensely satisfied. *Jouissance* is "bliss" (and also "orgasm"), and it describes more engaged reading—something I describe to my students as "the joy of grappling with a text and its ideas."

Rosenblatt describes her framework as "reading stances." There is efferent and aesthetic reading. Efferent reading is read-

---

1 a lot of different things, actually, because I'm a millennial and will never recover from the 2008 recession and student debt crisis, so I have to hold a minimum of three jobs at any given time.

ing that may or may not be boring or technical but is, at its core, designed to impart information or knowledge. When you read a recipe, you are reading efferently, because no matter how delicious all the description is, what the text is really there for is to let you know how many teaspoons of baking powder you need. Aesthetic reading covers just about everything else, and what I like about that is I can toss Barthes's distinctions inside it. That's how a dichotomous key works, right? Don't ask me; I'm not a naturalist, but I think that's how we did them in ninth-grade bio.

The reason I'm explaining all of this to you is because

1. I'd like tenure someday and I'd like to think trade publications matter even though they probably don't;
2. Jessica invited me to contribute to this anthology (and she is, no lie, at least 50 percent—probably more—responsible for my reading romance at all); and
3. I think it actually goes a long way to describe how and why I was resistant to reading romance, as well as how and why I changed my mind about it.

Let me explain.

People who know me get tired of hearing this pithy one-liner, but you and I don't know each other, so I can use it on you: I became a reader out of spite.

This is hyperbole, and I certainly didn't analyze it this way at the time, but it kind of explains a lot. My identity is a complicated story, but to just give you the Cliff's Notes: I'm biracial,

Black/white, Chicana, adopted, Jewish. That's a lot of things, and I didn't see myself in a lot of books growing up. And let me shut you up right there, Karen: I don't mean I was demanding books that covered literally all those points in one character. But there weren't a whole lot of children's books with even one of those facets of my identity represented, let alone something intersectional. Yet I LOVED to read. (And actually, Black girls and Black women are consistently at the top of the pack when it comes to running the numbers on who reads the most and who buys the most books, so you're welcome for the money, publishing, and fuck you, we deserve better. You're welcome to consult Pew, NPR, or a number of other sources for confirmation.) I think one of the things that drove me to keep reading—and that made me write my own stories—was that sense of dissatisfaction. If the book I had just finished denied my existence or multidimensional identity, maybe the next one wouldn't.

In seventh grade, I got this idea that all the books I loved reading were immature and that nobody would take me seriously if I didn't start reading "adult books." Instead of going to a librarian who might have introduced me to actual, good YA literature or at least done a good reader's advisory interview, I took this project on by myself. *Memoirs of a Geisha* was a hit that year, so that went on the short list, as did *Gone with the Wind* because my sister and I enjoyed watching the movie and she had loved the book. And then I browsed the local used bookstore, bravely leaving the children's section behind and going to the General Fiction section (this was before *Twilight* and only about halfway through Harry Potter, so nobody was yet making teen sections in stores).

I can't tell you which book I picked up first, but I can tell you that after I read one or two, I looked at the spines and put together that this publisher, one Red Dress Ink[2], was putting out the only books I was actually enjoying, because what kind of thirteen-year-old actually enjoys *Memoirs of a Geisha*? Their colophon became a touchpoint, a comfort, something I could rely on to be both engaging and aspirational—someday I, too, would be a young twentysomething, living in New York City, probably working in publishing, sleeping around, and eating ice cream straight out of the carton like a properly depressed girl (I also, around this time, watched *Bridget Jones's Diary* and aspired to be like her—later I realized it was not a good thing—still later I realized I *am* her, just Black, Latina, and Jewish). When I learned later on that it was chick lit and I was supposed to be as embarrassed of reading it as I should be to read the "immature" stuff I was running from, I really did not know what to do, so I kind of stopped reading.

Now, I am a book person, so what is "not reading" for me is not literally "not reading," but I would say the volume dropped by two-thirds, at least. That's a gigantic dip, and my enjoyment of reading dropped even more. Sure, every girl hides their Judy Blume or issue of *Cosmopolitan*, but I was reading books about adults and adult issues, and shouldn't that be something to be proud of? Wasn't that IMPRESSIVE?

---

2 Since acquired and reissued by Harlequin, I discovered while writing this essay—cut to me buying a bunch of the titles I remember reading and realizing I have absolutely no time to read them.

No. Just as The Baby-Sitters Club was inferior compared to whatever had won the Newbery Medal, *See Jane Date* was inferior to . . . I dunno, when I started at a college prep school for eighth grade, we read *Deathwatch*, *Romeo and Juliet*, and *The Way to Rainy Mountain*, so that, I guess? Why let a kid enjoy what they're reading when you could make them read about someone their age dying instead? *Confessions of a Shopaholic* is vapid and lowbrow, while a white woman questionably "adopting" a Native child while on some kind of desert spirit quest[3] is High Literature.

Speaking of binaries, here's another one: books are either Literary or they are Not. And my entire life as a reader has been spent negotiating that divide.

I studied creative writing in undergrad, and my fiction TA once gave me the grandest of compliments: "This story veered YA, but you really saved it in the end and kept it literary."

Thanks?

I actually *was* flattered, because I "knew" YA was juvenile and low quality, and I wanted to be a Serious Writer, and nobody would take me seriously if I wrote anything for teenagers.

White college sophomore who had never been out of the country, writing a story about traveling to savage South Africa, where they go on safari and speak Swahili? Literary brilliance. (And I was an uncooperative workshop bitch for pointing out that they speak about a thousand languages in South Africa,

---

3 Is that what *The Bean Trees* is about? I don't remember, because it was EXCRUCIATING, and not even my hometown being the setting could save it from being boring.

none of which are Swahili, and if you want to go on safari, you should try Kenya, because South Africa is basically in Antarctica.) Me, writing a throwaway line about a Black girl being annoyed that she spent hours straightening her hair only to see the baby hairs start to curl again when she started sweating? Completely incomprehensible; requires context and explanation; sounds too niche to be Literary.

Thankfully, I survived college, though obviously I harbor much resentment, and the next few years were actually wonderful, intellectually and bookishly speaking. I got a master's degree in children's literature, which means I was surrounded by a bunch of people who both loved the books I did and, possibly more importantly, put up with all the derision that comes when you tell people what you study and it's a thing they don't respect. I also got a master's degree in library science, which means I learned some of our immutable tenets, like how nobody should be shamed for their reading tastes. I learned a lot of words (and therefore meanings, contexts, movements, and frameworks) like *intersectional* and *privilege* and *whiteness* and *misogyny*, and how to wield them responsibly and powerfully.

So then when I looked back at my middle school ventures to the adult fiction section, I didn't feel shame or embarrassment for reaching out for chick lit—I felt shame and embarrassment because it was so white, so not-feminist, so fatphobic, so absurdly unrealistic about publishing salaries and New York City apartment sizes.

That is, I traded my Literary Quality–based snobbery for Wokeness-based snobbery.

That's, like, one ounce better, only because at least I earned that snobbishness from a lifetime of racial microaggressions.

And let's be fair—chick lit is problematic and white.

Another thing this essay is not about is why children's and young adult literature in particular needs to be diverse and representative for myriad reasons, but that's my discipline, so hit me up sometime and we'll discuss. Another Cliff's Notes: young readers who don't see themselves in books have markedly different senses of self-worth and a more limited view of their own future than kids who see themselves all over. Conversely, kids who see only themselves, and not people different from them, grow up to be assholes, less tolerant individuals. The reason that matters, in the context of this essay, is that typically kids grow up to become adults, and some adults read romance, and romance is hella white.

The most uninteresting thing in the world applies here: I thought romance was all Fabio, and traditional gender roles, and white, blond damsels, and dumbed-down prose, and lowbrow, formulaic nonsense, just as thousands of other people do. But then something happened. First of all, I met the editor of this anthology here, and she talked about romance so often I knew my perception had to be wrong, because Jessica Pryde is fucking brilliant, so if she's reading something, it must be both good and worth my time. I also just spent more time with book people and librarians, and a large swath of those people are intelligent and value multiple genres, so again, I must be wrong.

Finally—and crucially—I realized that the frequent jabs at how formulaic, dumbed down, or less complex the stuff I studied (children's and YA; please keep up) were very similar to the ones I and other people were lobbing at romance. How can I profess to be dedicated to convincing people that what I like and read has value if I was going to deny that to other readers? And how dare I assume that because a couple of romance novels are silly, that must be representative of an entire genre? I am constantly asking people not to do that with children's and YA books. Also, if you shed (inasmuch as that's even possible) your ingrained perception of what Literary Fiction looks like, you might notice that a lot of that shit is also formulaic and tired—do we really need another "I'm a cis hetero white dude with daddy issues, and that's why I cheated on my wife with my barely legal intern" Great American Novel? In the words of Vamp Willow, bored now.

Between befriending more and more people who read or write (or both, obvs) romance over the years, I began to suspect that maybe there was more to romance than I had initially thought. Then again, the Woke Person in me knew, from glancing at covers and knowing how the publishing industry works overall, that it was still going to be hella white. But it still deserved the benefit of the doubt, and what was there to lose about trying a book or two? A few hours of my time? I'm busy, but I'm not so busy I can't work a couple of them into my reading rotation.

Then again, did I really want to take all this time to explore something if it was going to be super white, just as children's and YA was finally starting to diversify, and just as I was deep enough into the industry to really know people and products—to have my finger on the pulse of everything? I know plenty about what different imprints do, which reviewers I trust, which agents represent which authors, and who is persona non grata. That saves a lot of time and headache in deciding what to read next. In the adult world, including romance? No idea. I'm not a book professional there, I'm just a reader.

Here's a "Two Kinds of People" framework I made up: there are people who read for wish fulfillment and people who read for affirmation. If you'd like to follow me along this dichotomous key I started making earlier, you could imagine this binary emerging under plaisir, but you could also make an argument for jouissance. Or both. Or we could just toss the dichotomy metaphor altogether.

I'm more of an affirmation person. As might already be evident, I harbor a lot of resentment from a lifetime of reading and schooling. And, like literally everyone, I have had my share of hard times and disappointments and everything else, stuff you cry about on the shoulder of your friends, siblings, or parents. I don't know about you, but "it'll be okay" or "this will work out" or "things happen for a reason" or "I know good things are around the corner" are not soothing to me. They inspire wrath, actually. Do you have a crystal ball and know for a fact that I'm about to experience something incredible? No? Then shut the fuck up. I don't need your toxic positivity, and I don't feel heard if you sit there listening to me express something complex and then give me a generic platitude in response.

(I suspect there's a pretty simple psychology explanation here, that people feel uncomfortable when someone around them is sad, and if they feel unequipped to solve a problem, they resort to platitudes. I can respect that it's awkward, but fuck you.

"I honor your pain" or "I'm sorry you are experiencing that; here are ways I can help you find the support you need" or just a truthful "I'm honestly at a loss here, but I am very sorry you are experiencing this" go a much longer way. It's very nice of you to feel bad for me, but your good wishes and hopes for me have zero to do with reality. I'd rather not hear them.)

I want people to see themselves mirrored in books, because they deserve that, but I want their *experiences* to be honored, not just their identities. I get frustrated when YA books end with the girl finally getting the guy or finally going to the top college she wanted to go to because those things don't—and didn't—happen. If I want a world of infinite possibilities, I can turn to fantasy. Realistic fiction is for reality.

So everything about romance seemed out of step with my orientation as a reader. Happily ever after? I don't know her. Also, everything I knew about romance from outside it was white girls at manors, wearing pretty dresses and falling in love with stable boys when they were actually betrothed to lords. What could I possibly get out of that?

Depending on how entrenched you are in the *social* books world, not just the *reading* books world, you may be familiar with our gripes on how New Adult Was Supposed to Be a Thing. This was a proposal for books that were "like" YA but with characters a bit older, like in their twenties, but that were distinct from romance or chick lit. *rolls eyes and shrugs* It was a totally legitimate ask, because YA is doing some incredible stuff, on the literary and commercial sides alike, but it's not like the second you're old enough to vote, you shed all your angst and are instantly welcomed into the adult world. A lot of what goes on in a lot of YA books, people were pointing out, was more typical of people in their early twenties, so why not publish books that recognize that? But then there were a lot of think pieces about how YA is garbage, how people need to grow the fuck up, and yadda yadda yadda (cf. all that shit about Great American Novels I said earlier), and then some people started calling their books New Adult even though the only part of that criteria they hit was the age of the protagonist, and everything burned down and it was dead before it had arrived.

So we had two choices, neither one sufficient: diverse YA that recognized a lot of twentysomething problems but did it with characters that were younger than that, and which was digging into the adult portion of their market a little too deeply instead of catering to the Actual Teenagers (which is a problem), or older white dudes living their worst lives.

Then I discovered this thing called Contemporary Romance, and I learned that while it, too, had its origins in white girl problems, it was grappling with that and so much more (like better disability, queer, and non-Christian religion rep; like recognizing trauma and triggers; like responding to today's economy and political landscape without expressly referencing specific events or presidents) in much the same way the kid lit and YA world was. All of a sudden, I was hearing names like Alyssa Cole, Jasmine Guillory, Alisha Rai, Suzanne Park, Mia Sosa, Priscilla Oliveras. I was hearing about a professional organization that had a huge membership, that was beloved by its members and also highly and publicly criticized when it fucked up (which is no small feat, actually). I was literally meeting some of these people at conferences and parties and getting to know them as brilliant, funny, introspective, critical, warm women[4] who shared many of my non-book interests and passions.

If those were the people making the books, those were the books I needed to read.

Did you know college-educated Black women are the biggest readers in America? It's weird, then, that books so rarely reflect us. You're welcome, publishing industry, for making you money, and also, fuck you for not serving us.

For a genre that was, I assumed, all about the wish fulfillment side of the dichotomy, contemporary romance was surprisingly affirming.

Time for another dichotomy! There are two types of kissing movies: love stories and romance. I didn't know this. Now I do. Love stories do not necessarily have happy endings, while romance movies always do, because romance adheres to specific rules, one of which is Happily Ever After. I don't know which one I prefer, so I guess they're tied for first, and that may explain why I've come around to contemporary Contemporary Romance (by which I mean "contemporary romance" published recently, not older stuff. I have not, to my knowledge, read any books in the contemporary romance vertical published before 2010. Not on purpose, but because it's just what I've found).

---

4 No, it's not only cis women who write romance, but it happens to be these cis women I met or encountered in booklists most frequently at the beginning.

That sounds like it makes no sense, but I think what I'm trying to tell you is that I think love stories are the Literary Fiction of the cinema world, while rom-coms are the Romance. (Remember, I'm talking about their place in the cultural hierarchy, not my personal feelings about them.) Love stories are epic and tragic, like *Titanic*. Or basically anything that takes place during wartime. (Typically white) protagonists are exceptional, standouts in their society, because they are the only person interested in dismantling gender roles or the only antiwar activist or the only person with past trauma or the only queer person for miles or the least racist or whatever.

I think that's what I was expecting romance novels to be, so I was preemptively uninterested. I'M NOT LIKE OTHER GIRLS is a super-tired trope, especially because love stories, still overwhelmingly white, are full of those girls. They're not uncommon at all! White people think they are exceptional, and they're really not. They're honestly kind of boring.

You see this in dystopian and post-apocalyptic novels, too. "Omg, what if our children were stolen and taken to weird schools against their and our will!?" say the whites, wringing their hands while Native peoples of North America side-eye them. "Wouldn't it be terrible if teenagers went to prison instead of rehabilitation, especially for nonviolent crimes?" they say, while the nation's Black and brown youth don't respond because they're too busy going in and out of the prison industrial complex. "Minority women have tons of babies and never know who the fathers are," say righteous, judgmental white people who make romantic comedies about upper-middle-class, sexually active white women (with full-time jobs and health insurance that undoubtedly includes birth control!?) who accidentally get pregnant and don't know whether it's the child of the hot bad boy or the wholesome hometown old flame.

I reluctantly started picking up contemporary romance novels by and starring women of color, and those are the things that actually do seem Not Like Other Girls—not because they were unlike real girls but because they were unlike all the other adult protagonists I was finding everywhere in the literary world or in the YA category, literary or commercial.

There are different ways that can manifest, including but not limited to

1. Girl with cute, quirky job—but with terrible remuneration (unlike that trope in white people, which inexplicably allows for huge apartments), and she constantly has to contend with that because money is real and she doesn't have family wealth to fall back on

2. Girl with very impressive high-powered career (C-suite executive, college professor, lawyer, politician) who is brilliant but has to constantly put up with white people's shit, which is real as fuck

3. New Adult girl who is just trying to figure her shit out, which is also real as fuck

4. Girl with past trauma that is not just generically traumatic but was actually made possible or exacerbated by racial, ethnic, socioeconomic, and sociocultural circumstances

I am finally seeing myself and my friends on the page.

Jasmine Guillory's Alexa is no less Black just because she's hooking up with a white man, and her Nik and Carlos prove that interracial relationships actually don't require a white person at all—and can still be interracial! Talia Hibbert's Dani Brown is a grad student and college instructor, and Alexa Martin's Marlee has a master's degree, which are all things going on in my life! Alyssa Cole writes about literal princesses without a feudal Europe-style setting, so maybe it IS possible for me to be a princess someday, too! Alexis Daria's Latina is kind of shitty at Spanish even though she hears and uses it all the time, while Farrah Rochon's Samiah lives and dies by social media, which . . . same, gurl, same (x2).

I like these stories because the romance is hard won. There are a lot of things standing in their way, and they are real things that affect women of color far more often and in different ways than they affect white women. We're more likely to have student debt, lower salaries, racist landlords, health problems, and so on. So even those tropes in romance, the things that non-romance readers often point to as reasons it's a lesser literature, are fresh. If anything, they're not tropes, because they are much more realistic than when those same things happen to white people. We don't see them all that often, so they're not tired, and I can identify with them because those protagonists don't fail upward.

I'll repeat: BIPOC protagonists don't fail upward. They absolutely cannot, partly because the rules of romance require that they not fail in the end, and partly because that's not what happens in real life. We have a lot more at stake, which gives a text a real tension, something that really just feels manufactured and shiny in the same stories starring white people. We have to be twice as good to get half as much (hey, have you missed dichotomies? That is not one, but because there are twos in it, it almost feels that way, and there's a literary term in my Bedford that would describe such a thing, but I forget what it is).

I have a very shitty track record when it comes to romance IRL, and I read for affirmation, not wish fulfillment, so it's taken me a long time to come around to this: contemporary romance starring women of color has broken my dichotomous key. It is affirming and it is aspirational, and while some days it makes me want to die because I'm still single, many days the verisimilitude makes me think I might have something to look forward to.

(Black) Love Is . . .
(Black) Love Ain't

DA'SHAUN HARRISON

Black Love Matters." This is a statement we have heard a lot of, especially in recent years, but what does it actually mean? Perhaps it does matter. I don't know that I care to argue that it doesn't entirely, but what does it mean for Black Love to matter? Black Love matters to whom? What is the cost of this love? Does Black Love matter because we believe it's important to be in relationship to/with people who share our experience in the World, or does it matter because it's revolutionary? If the former, that's an argument I'm willing to defend, albeit it is one that must, too, be complicated. But if it's the latter, if Black Love matters solely because it is supposed to be some sort of stand-in for—rather than a commitment to—"revolution" or "freedom" simply because Black people exist in relationship to one another, that's not something I am willing to place any value in.

If I had to define Black Love, I think I would say that it is, on the surface, a commitment to someone who is—or multiple people who are—Black. Partner(s), family, friends, strangers. But I think, more than that, it is a commitment to Black freedom, to the destruction of the conditions under which the Black is subjugated. In this way, I see Black Love not just as the existence of Black subjects in relationship to each other, but also as an entity that should necessitate the destruction of anti-Blackness on which a need for Black Love exists. I don't believe it functions in this way, however. It would be ideal if Black Love could be both an embodied praxis and a call to action, but since it is conceived by way of anti-Blackness, reproducing the harmfulness that necessitates its existence, this intervention is decidedly one from which many are still excluded.

Said again, if the concept of the Black was not predicated on the subjugation and objectification of so-called Black people, there would be no need for the concept of Black Love. For this form of love to be an "embodied praxis and a call to action," there must first be something for us to resist, something stifling our freedom that would therefore cause us to find refuge outside the scope of a hegemonized form of/way to love. Black Love could and should be the ideology that behooves the Black subject to study and embody revolution. If we love our partners, our family, our friends, and Black people generally, we should want them to be able to experience life. This love should lead us to a commitment against re-creating or actively participating in anti-Black violence. Instead, it works to placate or pacify those who even have the ability to experience it.

The real talk on this is that, in a structural sense and as it relates to romance, Black Love—in its most basic form—is most often reserved for a particular type of Black person. It's most often reserved for Black people who are thin, light-skinned, non-disabled, cisgender, heterosexual, Christian, and/or moneyed. This is how we define who is and is not Desirable, and as such, who does and does not deserve to experience love. That does not mean that Black folks who do not embody one or more of these identities don't experience love; many have, but it does mean that there is an exception to every rule and yet the rule determines the landscape for how the game must be played.

Beauty and Desire both determine so much about how we experience the World. Who generally gets access to housing, who generally gets access to employment, who generally gets access to health care—and who is able to use that health care to be properly diagnosed by medical professionals—and who generally gets access to love are all determined by one's proximity to or positionality inside of Desire. Many of us who sit at the intersections of dark-skinned, fat, Black, trans, queer, and/or disabled identities are often forced to consider whether or not we will ever experience romantic love, forced to wonder if that could ever be a possibility in a World that consistently tells us that we are not enough, that our existence is a nuisance, and that we must change in unrecognizable ways to even be offered the choice to be loved.

Some of us don't ever get the happily ever after. Some of us are always the Shrek with no Fiona, the Beast with no Beauty, the frog who never transforms into royalty, the Fat Albert— assigned always to caregiver and never to a receiver of care. Some of us are the people for whom love doesn't shape-shift; the people for whom love doesn't make room; the people for whom time doesn't stand still and magical creatures don't concoct magical potions for us to experience a reality where we are more than Ugly. And love, in this way, is created as something, and some Thing, that requires that one be in proximity to Beauty to be loved. Shrek could only be with Fiona if she was an ogre, or if he was a prince, but Fiona had to have first been a princess.

The Beast was transformed from a prince to a beast as a form of punishment—an ailment curable only by falling in love with "a beautiful young woman." His Beastliness was never to be understood as a good thing, or something that didn't need to be transformed; rather, it was to be understood as a response to his inability to offer love, and the only thing that could teach him how to love was this beautiful young woman. Love was only possible if he was able to convince someone that his Ugliness was worth loving, even as he understood that one day his Beauty would be returned to him. The Beauty is twofold here, and the stipulations for the love he is supposed to embody are predicated on his connection to—and love's entanglement with—Beauty.

The lesson for this story is usually taught in one way: love can transform anyone, and in fact, one must transform in order to experience love. This lesson, however, is already blemished. If interrogated deeper, what it suggests is that for one to experience love, they must first be Beautiful. In this movie, just before the Beast is about to take his dying breath, Belle professes her love for him and he is restored to his humanness and thus his Beauty. The greater lesson, then, is that those rendered Ugly can experience only death; we can experience the ability to perhaps take pleasure in existing in proximity to love, but never the experience of freedom that one is promised comes with love. That love, the love that is supposed to break curses and release us from shackles, is reserved only for those who are positioned as Beautiful. The prince was transformed from a white Human to a dark beast and, after ten years and nearing what would soon be his death, crossed paths with the only thing that could save him: another white Human, which must always be understood as the standard for Beauty.

In my book, *Belly of the Beast: The Politics of Anti-Fatness as Anti-Blackness*, I define Desire/ability to complicate how we understand Desire—and thus, the structural violence of both Beauty and Ugliness:

> *Desire/ability politics and Desire Capital, however, suggest that one does not need to feel pretty to be Pretty; one does not need to feel beautiful to be Beautiful; one does not need to feel ugly to be Ugly. How one benefits or suffers from the subjugation of particular people is not determined by their feelings; it is determined by the identities they embody.*
>
> *Desire/ability politics is the methodology through which the sovereignty of those deemed (conventionally) Attractive/Beautiful is determined. Put another way, the politics of Desire labels that which determines who gains and holds both social and structural power through the affairs of sensuality, often predicated on anti-Blackness, anti-fatness, (trans)misogynoir, cissexism, queer antagonism, and all other structural violence. It is intended to name*

the social, political, and economic capital one obtains / is given access to through their ability to be Desire. By this I mean that Desire is about much more than being desired; it is about one's ability to always already be positioned as the very embodiment of the thing(s) that make(s) one Desire/able.

ACCORDING TO BELL hooks, as she writes in *All About Love*, love is composed of several different ingredients: "care, affection, recognition, respect, commitment, and trust, as well as honest and open communication." She offers that one of these ingredients can be present without the others, but for it to be love—real and true—they must all be present at once because love cannot exist in the same space as negligence and abuse. I posit that if this is true, if we agree with hooks's understanding of love, then so much about what we understand as love actually isn't. Most commonly, love is portrayed as abusive, tough, and hard. Through social institutions like media, family, school, and religion, we are taught that love requires that we be beaten and broken, that we be torn apart, either by words or by hand. We are taught that circumstances like infidelity are normal. We are forced into violent gender(ered) roles that produce a hierarchy in our relationships, positioning one party over the other. All of this is violent, and it is violence, and the sting of this harm festers and grows even through identities we are taught are supposed to disrupt this norm. Homonormativity, or this idea that LGBTQ+ spaces and relationships should reproduce the same violent heteronormative ideals homogenized by society, comes to mind. All of this exists in opposition to the way hooks defines love. There is no care, or respect, or commitment, or communication there. Only harm, abuse, violence, and dishonesty.

As I understand it, and as has been previously stated, the World is predicated on the subjugation of the Black—positioning us always and already as the Other. Abuse and negligence, then, are foundational to an anti-Black world, making love an impossibility for the Black. Nothing other than destroying the conditions that engender anti-Blackness can change this truth. This means that not only is love an impossibility, but it is also something we should not desire—at least in the way it has been homogenized. Hortense Spillers, professor and brilliant Black Feminist scholar, once stated that "unless one is free, love cannot and will not matter." I want to parse this statement. If the idea is that love is supposed to save us from the violence of the World, I agree that love does not matter. It can't. In so many ways, it has stifled our desire to break free from the hold of anti-Blackness. And yet, many do not define love in this same way. And for those for whom love has been inaccessible, the idea that it does not matter at all feels incomplete. For those who desire it, they deserve to be held. From this, I infer that many desire touch, intimacy, togetherness, and sacred community, and it is so often conflated with love.

I believe this is the intervention phrases like "Black Love" seek to make. Whether we refer to it as Black Love or something else, Black folks have long found ways to exist in partnership with one another where grace and attentiveness abound—even as we are forced to work within the confines of colonialism's linguistic limitations. As this is the case, I understand Black Love to be an acknowledgment of the ways that love has failed the Black and an attempt to curate something that holds us in love's place. It is this attempt at being held outside of love, even as it is still described as love, that those who are positioned as Ugly—or who cannot access Beauty—are removed from. How can Black Love be the entity that creates room for Black subjects to love, with all its limitations, if the Black fat is excluded? If the Black queer is reduced only to sex and not their ability to be intimate in myriad ways? If the Black trans person can only ever be a fetish one takes part in and not a living being one gives love to? What is the utility of Black Love if disabled persons are requested, or demanded, to "cure" or hide their disabilities? If this intervention of the colonial, anti-Black logics of love itself only reproduces, or reifies, those very same violences, it's something we must move away from.

This is not to say there are not exceptions to the rule. There are Black fat, queer, trans, and/or disabled people who do experience this iteration of love. And that there is a rule for there to be exceptions to is indicative of the much larger issue being written about here. Many of us want to be cared for, held, heard, engaged honestly and earnestly, and affirmed in a particular way, and we know that as love. We have created and ascribed to Black Love as a sort of reimagining of these actions without the violence assigned to the way love has been homogenized. But colonial violence, anti-Black violence, cannot be "reimagined." In order to not replicate it, it can only be destroyed.

Black Love Matters insofar as it's essential that we build and maintain community with each other. But for as long as Blackness does not cohere, which is to say for as long as there is a race project that sustains anti-Blackness, Black Love will also always be limited.

(Black) Love is prohibiting . . . (Black) Love ain't freeing.

Black Love is an intercession . . . Black Love ain't a liberatory ideology.

Love is violent . . . Black Love ain't the revolutionary act we've claimed it to be.

(Black) Love is . . . (Black) Love ain't.

Black Indie Romance

CHRISTINA C. JONES

Black Indie Romance is the baddest chick in the room.

Dressed to the nines—maybe a little inappropriately, but really, who's to say?

Those whose names "belong" on the list sneer at her, wondering how she could have snuck in. The true, hard-core fans recognize her. They smile when they see her there, feeling proud of the fact that they supported her before the "mainstream" knew her name or saw her face.

While everybody else is whispering, picking apart her flaws, snickering behind their hands about her unworthiness, all the ways she's not like them, not as good as them . . . She stands strong.

Confident.

Knowing that if nothing else . . . The room is talking about her, even if later they swear they have no idea who she is.

If that analogy is a stretch to you, maybe you haven't been paying attention to the romance landscape. Through the years, romance has struggled to find its place in the literary community, often overlooked or looked down upon for largely centering the lives—and more importantly, the happiness—of its female characters.

Over and over, we've seen articles in huge publications deriding romance as formulaic, crass, and unworthy of respect as serious literature. These articles are filled with outdated references to Fabio and ripped bodices (both of which are perfectly fine) instead of focusing on the way the genre has evolved to be more inclusive—and more feminist.

While every genre has its problematic elements, gone are the days where slut-shaming, queerphobia, xenophobia, and racism are mainstays in most romance novels. By no means are all—or even most—romance novels a safe place for the identities that make up our multifaceted world and readership. I do believe the space is much safer than it used to be.

But there is still plenty of work to do.

Romance has never had a problem with popularity among readers, even when said readers wouldn't dare admit to its consumption. I won't pretend to have the hard numbers about this, but I know that romance is a huge moneymaking business.

I've even seen arguments that among genre fiction it is *the* moneymaking business.

And I believe we're starting, finally, to earn some of the respect that goes hand in hand with those dollars. It's a slow-going process, but romance is also becoming more inclusive of the full fabric of humanity. All different races, ethnicities, gender identities, sexualities, all are finding it still not easy enough, but easier to see themselves between the pages of sweeping love stories that make the happiness and companionship we all deserve seeing even more real.

And it's not solely being left up to big, traditional publishing, either.

A huge part of the diversification of the landscape has come in the form of writers who have taken hold of the reins themselves, writing and pursuing the business of publishing as independent entities.

As with most things, Black women, as much as we can, have not allowed ourselves to be excluded or erased from that narrative either.

For whatever reason (we know the reason), Black indie romance authors are not embraced in the same manner as women we've looked up to and considered our peers. It's rare for us to get the same magazine spread mentions, the "bookstagram" and "booktube" features, the typical "Romancelandia" excitement about our covers featuring Black couples. Still, indie romance writers who keep their focus on representing Black love as the center of their work are still pressing forward, because we understand that notoriety is not what makes our work and our voices valuable.

It is simply our existence that does this.

Close your eyes for a moment and think about Black love.

What visual does that bring to mind for you?

Maybe it's a little cheesy or corny, but really, I want you to do it—I want you to think about Black people, together. And I'm not even talking about sexually—not to minimize the importance of that—but I mean . . . the romance, the intimacy, the togetherness and community of two (or maybe more) people who have been historically told that they're unattractive, unworthy, unwanted, simply because of their race. Envision them finding themselves very much needed, very much desired, passionately yearned for, in the context of a society that still treats Black characters on-screen and on-page as if they're only as important as their proximity to whiteness.

I don't know about you, but that's powerful to me.

It's important.

It's necessary.

For me, the visual of Black love brings to mind laughing at classic Black movies together, quoting them at random and trusting that your partner is going to instantly pick up on the reference. And if they can't, that's cool, too, because it's an opportunity to introduce them to another unique part of the diverse landscape of Black art.

It's a foam plate and a red plastic cup, both protected against invading insects by a paper towel, handed to you at a family reunion because you were too busy catching up to get in line to grab a plate.

It's a hand reaching across the car to rest on and maybe even squeeze your thigh partway through a long drive, while the kids are asleep in the back seat on the way home.

It's warmth and familiarity.

It's resistance against a violent history that has seen families torn apart, from the horrific torture of slavery to the iniquity of mass incarceration and an unevenly wielded justice system that rips valuable pieces of family units from their homes.

It's beautiful.

And I'm so grateful—I'm honored—to be a part of the subsection of this romance industry that keeps our eyes focused on bringing that beauty to the page.

"BLACK IS NOT a genre."

I'll never, ever forget how hurtful it was to see that sentence on Twitter, and at the hands of a Black author who writes romance novels that feature Black characters—at least, I think so.

Obviously, I understand the sentiment of such a statement— it's a resistance to being labeled as "other," or having your work seen as only for a certain audience. It's a rejection against being boxed in by a limiting statement.

The thing is, though . . . I don't find the Blackness of my skin, my characters, or my work to be limiting. And truly, I'm insulted by the idea that it is.

So often, as authors—or as any creator seeking to make a living from their work—we're sold this idea of success coming from being appealing and accessible to the largest possible pool of customers. But when I look at . . . let's use luxury fashion brands as the example: they aren't appealing to everyone.

They are appealing to their customers.

The way I see it, Black romance authors who write Black characters face a non-dilemma. In a world where many—maybe most—of our neighbors can't publicly, comfortably say a phrase as simple as Black Lives Matter with no qualifiers or clarifications, should we really consider those same people part of our target audience?

My answer?

No.

There is very little reward in trying to force others to see your humanity—even less in convincing them that your happily ever afters are heartwarming, sexy, and realistic. There are those who want to be more inclusive than they actually are, so maybe they'll purchase to show the internet they're a "colorblind" ally. And, absolutely, there is a portion of the "mainstream" audience who are not Black but are truly interested in, and enjoy, Black love stories.

Is that number, taken as a whole, larger than the Black audience who is interested in your work? I'd love to see numbers supporting that, but until I do . . . I don't believe it. What I have seen are Black authors lamenting that their publisher put people of a different race—or no people at all—on their covers to "mask" the race of the characters between the pages. I've seen Black authors talk about their books with Black people on the covers not selling as well. I've seen publishers come under fire for quiet comments about how Black people don't sell.

And all this leads me to believe that . . . Black romance doesn't sell . . . to white people.

Black readers, though?

We adore it.

The Black women who converge on us at signings and conferences geared toward "us," their excited comments on social media, the way they push our books up the Amazon charts every time we release a new tale of Black love—they all love Black romance, and they cannot get enough of it.

At these events—like Girl, Have You Met, which was established by me and my friend and indie romance peer Alexandra Warren—we get countless thank-yous from women who've never been to anything like it. A room full of hundreds of Black people, celebrating relationships and love that look like what created us, what we live, what we dream of . . . it's the kind of thing that makes the late nights, early mornings, headaches, and tears all worth it.

Because the celebration of Black love means something to them.

That was why Alexandra and I created Girl, Have You Read (which focuses on the books, the same way the event focuses on meeting the authors) in the first place. There was no central place that would give indie authors any respect or attention that also put the celebration of Black relationships at center stage.

So instead of whining and complaining, trying to force ourselves into a space where we clearly weren't valued . . . we built it.

And they came.

And those readers show up for us, every single day.

So why in the world would they not be my target audience?

And why in the world would publishing ignore that?

Sure, maybe more "mainstream" romance has a wider appeal, but so do original Cheetos. I highly doubt the specialty flavors sell as well, but it doesn't keep the company from making them available to the people who love them.

They even put them right next to the other Cheetos—in their own box, for easy access for people who are looking for them; no one wants to dig around through a whole bin of one type of snack, looking for that lone copy of something that's different, but speaks more to specific taste buds.

So . . . maybe the publishing industry could take a few hints from the snack companies.

Back to what I referred to as a "non-dilemma," though.

Black women support Black romance—defined as a story focused on a relationship where all the people in that relationship are Black. Do Black women read other things—absolutely! We have incredibly diverse palates.

But we deserve to see the relationships that created us—the relationships that we coveted and observed growing up—and the relationships we're in reflected in this industry we love to consume.

In all pairings.

I believe that publishing has, slowly, been trying to make a change. But when it comes to showing us together . . . there's been a disappointing lack—and simultaneous gaslighting—that has been incredibly disheartening to witness. When you can have panels full of romance authors who happen to be Black, given an incredible stage to gush about their work, their characters, their readers, that's amazing!

But then you look at their covers and there are no Black faces.

Or a hot new book is coming out, and there is a Black woman on the cover . . . but she's the only one between those pages.

We're supposed to see it as progress.

I love that those Black authors are making their names in publishing, and getting the accolades and applause—I would never minimize their work, or the heart and effort they put into it. They deserve to be celebrated.

But it's not inspiring, for me.

Because what I see is, you can be Black, and win, as long as your characters aren't Black, too. Or if they are, maybe just one. As long as it's not too Black. As long as they don't use certain language. As long as they don't do certain things. As long as they're normal.

When publishing gives a Black woman who writes Black relationships the same press and promotion as it gives authors whose work focuses on majority non-Black leads—and that Black woman's work doesn't have to be filtered first through an "acceptable negro" sieve?

That will be progress to me.

I wonder what changed in the public consciousness that makes seeing Black people loving each other in popular media such an anomaly?

As far as I can tell, even the Black love interests in mostly white shows, movies, and books are presented as less of a whole, fully realized person, more as character development for the white people the show is really about. Yes, there are those where this isn't the case, but it's unfortunately prevalent. Much more visible than modern examples of Black people loving each other.

What is the message in that?

That Black people being loved is only as valid as the white person they're in the relationship with? But only, of course, if there isn't too much attention given to their Blackness—but really, that's a whole other topic.

The problem is not the existence or popularity of interracial romance. The problem is that instead of taking space from over-represented white narratives, Black romance gets pushed out. And we're expected to accept it as representative of something it is not. I have not, am not, and will not argue against interracial relationships having their time in the sun—those relationships are just as important and valid as any other.

What I don't accept, though, is being inundated with purple when I asked for blue.

Purple is fine.

But it is not blue.

This erasure didn't always exist—in fact, there was a time when interracial relationships were taboo in mainstream—it was a big deal. Viewers threatened to boycott *Star Trek*. Tom and Helen Willis were played for laughs against George Jefferson's snide comments. I'm not suggesting we go back to that; I'm wondering, instead, what the reasoning could be behind those relationships taking the place of the plethora of Black relationships that used to be so highly available on-page and on-screen.

It was not always this way.

As of sitting down for this article, I'm struggling to think of any "popular" mainstream Black romance authors—the kind white readers could name—whose work reflects even primarily Black relationships. Every time I run across these lists, every time someone is asked to name their favorite Black contemporary, 95 percent of the time, the name given is of an author whose work is mainly interracial.

That's not a knock against those authors.

It just makes me wonder if a white love interest—that the "mainstream" can "relate" to—is a requirement for publishing dollars. Yes, Black authors who write Black characters can get the book deal—but will they get the other things that make a book "successful"?

Will they get the catered signings, and panels with other authors gushing over their work? Will they get the coveted *NYT* Bestseller status, propelled by massive marketing budgets and creative promotions? Will advance review copies be sent not just to the big, notable places, but to the smaller Black reviewers and bloggers who are the backbone of the Black romance community? Some authors fight so hard against the idea of a "Black section," but without it, are publishers making sure we get shelf placement at all? I walk past the romance section at every store I enter that sells books. I've learned that the chances of seeing Black faces on more than maybe—big maybe—one or two covers is rare.

I believe that, maybe, I've questioned this too long.

Thought about it way too hard, only to arrive at a simple answer of racism and laziness, with a healthy dose of *they don't really see our humanity at all*.

I've thought about it so hard that I've wondered, why the hell are you thinking about this so hard? And . . . Why does it matter so much? And . . . Does it actually matter at all?

Well . . . yes.

To me, it does.

I grew up with the TV on in the background, welcoming me into the worlds of other—albeit fictional—people. The Evans family and their struggles to grow up in the projects, *Sanford and Son*, *The Jeffersons*—some of the earliest examples I can remember on TV. None of these shows gave me a particularly warm, fuzzy visual of Black love on-screen—in fact, they were a bit horrifying in their realism—but the drama and comedy and emotion of all of them paved the way for more "modern" Black TV.

The Cosby Show. A Different World. I won't wax too poetically about *The Cosby Show* for obvious reasons, but if I look solely to Cliff and Clair as fictional characters, they were game-changing for me as a child. This wealthy Black family who loved each other.

What a concept!

And then there was spinoff *A Different World*, which first introduced me to so many concepts—dorm life, sororities and fraternities, and . . . Black Love. I didn't know what that was back then, probably because it wasn't a big deal; it wasn't uncommon to see Black people in love with each other on TV. Ron and Freddie . . . Ron and Kim. Whitley and Dwayne. Plus all the other interpersonal relationships that happened in between. That show very much set the stage for me to see Black Love as normal, and desirable. Not flawless, or perfect.

But beautiful.

My entire world opened from there.

Hangin' with Mr. Cooper. Sister, Sister. The Fresh Prince of Bel-Air.

Mark Curry, Holly Robinson Peete, and Dawnn Lewis cycled through baddies, male and female, as the norm. Tia and Tamera kept a cute Black boyfriend—and I'll admit that even though they always wanted their annoying neighbor Roger to go home, I wanted him to come to my house.

Will, Carlton, Ashley, and Hilary?

Always with Black love interests.

Martin. Living Single. The Wayans Bros. The Jamie Foxx Show.

Introduced us to everybody in Black Hollywood—cameos left and right, as love interests and otherwise.

And I felt so seen.

Especially once Black TV came around to *Moesha, The Parkers,* then *Girlfriends, One on One, Half & Half.*

More recently?

The Game. Atlanta. Queen Sugar. Insecure.

These are the relationships I watched through my formative years, the experiences I internalized—good and bad—that made me feel seen on-screen. Black Love was never a last resort for these shows. It was the center, it was the lifeblood—and it took nothing away from any show where that wasn't the case. But they gave those of us who felt and appreciated that—who were looking for that—exactly what we needed.

We don't really have that anymore.

I already know, dear reader, that your brain is coming up with a list of shows that defy my words—of course there's not an absence of Black Love on TV—and you're about to prove it to me. But I want you to filter out any shows that didn't premiere within the last five years. I want you to filter out any that aren't a predominantly Black cast. And then, only show me the ones that are available outside of premium channels/streaming.

Yeah.

Exactly.

Because even if we include the shows from prestige TV and the streaming networks . . . the numbers just aren't great.

And they're even worse for books.

Of the last ten Black authors who earned the status of *New York Times* Bestseller, whose book centered a romantic relationship, how many of those didn't feature a white love interest?

Were there any?

No.

There were not.

Again—not at all a knock against those authors, but it feels pretty homogenous, right? When you take these books that are supposed to be about Black people, and you compare those relationships to the real-life statistics about Black Love . . . now do you see the point?

To get romantic storytelling that gives readers the same feeling as those shows I mentioned, one would have to turn their sights to books that haven't been filtered through the lens of an industry that doesn't appreciate—and certainly doesn't reward—the pairing of Black characters with each other.

If I want the soul, the nuance, the respect, the love of culture, the rejection of the white gaze, the full embrace of "Black on

Black" love, I have to go where all of that is given without reservation. I have to turn to authors who love Black women, who are proud to state that while anybody can read and enjoy the work, it's for us.

I have to turn to where Black is not only absolutely a genre, but a mainstay—an imperative. Not monolithic, not always stereotypical, but absolutely all-encompassing.

Black Indie Romance.

The baddest chick in the room.

I can go to Black Indie Romance to find absolutely anything I'd like to read, centering Black characters. I . . . could actually turn to my own catalog for many different genres, but honestly— I would be in great company, among other authors who are writing for Black women.

Our mentions of gray sweats and head wraps and door-knockers and fish plates don't have to be watered down, reworded, or explained; they are simply understood, because we're writing, to some degree, about the lives we lead. And when we expand those horizons beyond everyday people, into the paranormal or ultra-rich or dystopian, or whatever, those little Easter eggs—those tiny love letters to our Blackness—they still have a place.

When I'm writing, there are only rare moments of doubt over whether or not my audience will get it. Because my audience is . . . me. My audience is my friends, my peers, my sister, my mother, the woman I share a nod and a smile with in the grocery store because there are so few of us around town.

It's a beautiful kind of freedom, to me.

Freedom from pressure to make my work more accessible, more mainstream, more relatable to . . . the masses.

To white people.

To make it less . . . me.

It's my most sincere hope that one day soon, the publishing industry will see the value of some Black author who writes Black romance, and will give her all the resources she needs to access the readers who are hungry for work that makes them feel seen. I hope the industry doesn't dull or dilute the cultural references or specificity. I hope they don't water it down to make it palatable.

I hope they understand that they can set a new standard, instead of adapting to one built by centuries and decades of racist beliefs about how Black people connect with, relate to, and love on each other.

Just because something is the way it has always been, doesn't make it the way it always has to be.

That could be a pipe dream. Or it could be right around the corner—the very best of luck and well wishes to you, Sis, whoever you are, wherever you are, if you're reading this. Enjoy that time in the sun, and make it everything.

But in the meantime, until that happens—and while it's happening, because we aren't going anywhere—I know I can find all the warmth and support in the world among my people.

The Black Indie.

"We've been doing this a long-ass time"

A Postscript

In the early days of the COVID-19 pandemic, many bookstores and other organizations began to use technology that was growing more and more familiar to the world to bring authors to the masses, stuck in their homes or trapped in essential work that left them vulnerable to the whims of others. Loyalty Books, a Black- and woman-owned bookstore in Washington, DC, was one of those bookstores. Among other excellent programs centering the voices of diverse authors and other book people, Hannah O. Depp coordinated "Date Night with Alyssa Cole," a semi-regular Friday evening conversation featuring a rotating collection of romance authors.

To see a Black woman–owned bookstore embracing a regular romance-themed program curated by a Black romance author was a huge draw, and it continued to be throughout 2020 and into the following year. In one particular conversation that eventually landed on characters, settings, and experiences that are front and center in her novels, Beverly Jenkins (lovingly called Ms. Bev by her friends and fans) sighed, lit a cigarette, and declared, "We've been doing this a long-ass time."

She'd been talking about the Black authors who were her peers and her predecessors, but she was also talking about Black people in general. Black people who have dealt with the harsh and ridiculous features of a white supremacist culture that have led us to where we are today. Black people who continue to pave their own way because society—with publishing and greater entertainment media as a great cross section—finds new ways to make decisions that are dissonant with what the world is telling them.

Black readers and consumers who have long read books and watched movies that don't center characters like us in the most basic ways, and who sought that spark of light that comes with seeing ourselves in stories where good succeeds, love wins, and everyone lives happily ever after.

Black stories are everyone's stories.

Sure. Great. Wonderful.

But more important, they're our stories, and we all deserve the right to see ourselves in them.

Black people, in the United States and elsewhere, have been working to be seen in all the ways that matter for centuries. Whether it's being seen as a whole person, considered human enough to participate in regular society, or to be able to peacefully and quietly fall in love and get married, we have done all we can to retain our own humanity and our mental and emo-

tional health along with it. One of the ways we continue to remind ourselves of our own humanity is our ability to find and
keep romantic love, whatever we may consider it to be, or however important we might find it.

As I write this in late spring 2021, I think about the growing
number of people I see claiming their places, sharing their stories, and making their voices heard on behalf of their Black
brethren. Cis and trans, queer and straight, neurotypical and
neurodivergent, all broadening the world's enjoyment and understanding of what it is to be Black and in love, and the many
ways we can fall.

And I can't wait to see what you all do next.

Acknowledgments

There are so many people without whom this book wouldn't exist.

My infinite gratitude goes to my agent, Tara Gelsomino, for taking the time to listen and speak as a partially baked idea formed into a real concept, and for taking the time to make it a reality. Your support and encouragement, your never-ending font of ideas, and your persistence in getting this book into the right hands have been a wonder to watch and experience.

To Cindy Hwang, Angela Kim, Dache' Rogers, Fareeda Bullert, and the rest of the amazing team at Berkley, for seeing the importance of this topic and believing that this book could be a rare, but hopefully not the last, nonfiction book in their catalog. And to Monica Ahanonu, for sharing your amazing artistic gift with the world.

To Carole V. Bell, Sarah Hannah Gómez, Jasmine Guillory, Da'Shaun Harrison, Margo Hendricks, Adriana Herrera, Piper Huguley, Kosoko Jackson, Nicole M. Jackson, Beverly Jenkins, Christina C. Jones, Julie E. Moody-Freeman, and Allie Parker, for bearing with me as we worked to get this made, and for producing such amazing words. You are all inspiring human beings, and I am so grateful to have been given your time and wisdom for the past few years. And to those folks who were unable to contribute but offered encouraging words and support for the project—you'll never know how much that meant to me in the early days.

To Hannah especially, for believing, pushing, and cheering. I never would have opened that DM if you hadn't been there to ~~goad~~ encourage me. I've never been happier for a friendship meet-cute for the ages and an accountability partner who is also a beloved friend.

To Reneé, without whose steady encouragement and presence I would have melted down long ago. And to whom I owe several thousand iced raspberry chais for all the reading, brainstorm walks, conceptualizing, revising, and . . . everything else. And to everyone at Write Wednesday for their support and quiet tapping in the earliest days of proposal writing.

To Jen, for pushing me to use my disgustingly excessive amount of available time off, and everyone in CSO (yes, including you *again*, Reneé). There's no place I'd rather go (or not go) every day.

To every single person with whom I came into contact at Arizona Oncology—thank you for making an already difficult year just a little bit easier with your advice, support, friendly smiles, and top-notch care.

To everyone under the IPH umbrella, and especially to Dr. Early, for teaching me how to read deeply, ask questions, and evaluate my own understanding of the answers. Sometimes where we start is a long way from where we end up, but the whole journey can be enlightening.

To too many online friends to name, who inspired me to investigate and broaden my reading and who introduced me to some of the best people in the world. To the Black readers and writers who make me laugh, cry, think, and rethink on a regular basis on Twitter and elsewhere. To my Book Riot family especially, for being there to answer the strangest, most bizarre questions and provide never-ending cheerful, snarky, delightful support. My world is so much better and bigger thanks to the ways you've actively and passively given me joy.

To every Black woman who has encouraged me or pushed me, who sought to help me understand my worth—whether teachers, colleagues, friends, family, or that ubiquitous other— thank you for showing me who I could be and what I could do, even when I wasn't so sure myself.

To Brigette, for starting my romance discourse journey That Long Ago with the Montgomery Brothers and a red pen.

To my family on both sides of the country, for their confused but excited support and uplifting words. You've all gotten me to where I am today.

And to Mommy, who knows what she did.

Finally, to James, for not always knowing what I'm talking about in my constant, incessant chatter about romance novels and Twitter drama, but who always offers a shoulder, a snuggle, and a meal. I can probably guess who I might be without you, but I don't care to ever find out if it's true.

About the Contributors

Carole V. Bell is a cultural critic, communication scholar, and a lover of politics and popular culture. Her research investigates the connections between media, politics, and public opinion in the United States. She has been interviewed on NPR, WGBH, WCVB, FiveThirtyEight, and in *The Atlantic* and has written for print and online media including the *New York Times*, *BookPage*, Book Riot, *Publishers Weekly*, Shondaland, and The Grio. You can find excerpts and links to recent articles, interviews, and reviews at cvbell.com.

Carole earned a PhD in Mass Communication Research from the UNC–Chapel Hill School of Journalism and Media, a Master of Science in Television and Radio from Brooklyn College, and a B.A. in English and American Literature from Harvard University. Her forthcoming book analyzes the political and social meanings attached to interracial romance in American film.

Sarah Hannah Gómez was born and raised in Tucson, Arizona, where she lives now. She holds an MA in children's literature and MS in library science from Simmons College and is currently a doctoral candidate at the University of Arizona, studying children's and young adult literature with a minor in social, cultural, and critical theory. Formerly a librarian, she pivoted careers to become a fitness instructor and now works at Kevin Anderson & Associates as the publishing industry's first ever in-house senior editor of cultural accuracy and sensitivity reading.

Jasmine Guillory is the *New York Times* bestselling author of six romance novels, including *The Wedding Date*, *The Proposal*, and *While We Were Dating*. Her work has appeared in *O, The Oprah Magazine*, *Cosmopolitan*, *Bon Appétit*, and *Time*. She lives in Oakland, California.

Da'Shaun Harrison is a Black trans writer, abolitionist, and community organizer in Atlanta, Georgia. Harrison currently serves as the managing editor of *Wear Your Voice* magazine and is the author of *Belly of the Beast: The Politics of Anti-Fatness as Anti-Blackness*. Harrison is also a public speaker who often gives talks and leads workshops on Blackness, queerness, gender, fatness, disabilities, and the intersection at which they all meet.

Harrison's tenure as a community organizer in Atlanta began in 2014 during their first year at Morehouse College. Along with several other student organizers, Harrison helped build a student-led organizing body named AUCShutItDown. The group's work was centered around police violence in Metro Atlanta, gentrification, campus-based sexual violence, and queer/trans-antagonistic school policies. In 2015, that work expanded to the creation of

Atlanta Black Students United—a collective of Black student organizers from colleges and universities across Metro Atlanta dedicated to restructuring the policies and cultures of their respective campuses. In 2016, following the uprisings birthed by the murders of Alton Sterling and Philando Castile, Harrison and four other Black queer and trans organizers created #ATLisReady. AiR, as it was called, sought to consolidate already-existing work moving across the city, and to make it easier for community organizers to network with one another.

Harrison penned their first published piece in the summer of 2017 while navigating heightened poverty and homelessness. This would become the genesis of their writing career. Harrison writes not only as a means of survival but with the belief that if the marginalized wish for a future where their history is depicted accurately and their stories are told correctly, then they must document them. Writing, for Harrison, is not solely a passion or talent, but is the foundation on which their home—their love, their survival, their creativity—is built. It is their expression of self, their contribution to the documentation of the histories of oppressed/colonized peoples.

Harrison's writing has appeared in and on PhiladelphiaPrint, Medium, them., Black Youth Project, BET, and other online publications. They have also been featured in/interviewed by *The Fader*, Everyday Feminism, BuzzFeed, *Teen Vogue*, the *New York Times*, and other local and national publications.

Find out more about Harrison on their website: dashaunharrison .com.

Margo Hendricks is professor emerita of Renaissance and Early Modern English Literature at the University of California, Santa Cruz. She has published extensively on race, Shakespeare, and early modern English literature and culture. Her academic book, *Race and Romance: Coloring the Past*, is forthcoming with ACMRS Press. As Elysabeth Grace, she has written a paranormal series, Daughters of Saria, and a contemporary Black romance, *Your Heart Only*. She is presently at work on a "Black love" historical romance set in sixteenth-century England.

Adriana Herrera, a *USA Today* bestselling author, was born and raised in the Caribbean, but for the last fifteen years has let her job (and her spouse) take her all over the world. She loves writing romance centering Afro-Latinx culture and joy. Her work has received starred reviews from *Publishers Weekly* and *Booklist* and has been featured on NBC's *Today* show and in the *New York Times*, *O, The Oprah Magazine*, *Entertainment Weekly*, NPR, *Library Journal*, and the *Washington Post*. She's a trauma therapist in New York City, working with survivors of domestic and sexual violence.

Piper Huguley is a two-time RWA Golden Heart finalist and is the author of Migrations of the Heart, a three-book series of historical romances set in the early twentieth century, featuring African American characters.

Huguley is also the author of the Home to Milford College series. The series follows the building of a fictitious college from its founding in 1866. The contemporary romance novel in this series,

Sweet Tea, was published by Hallmark Publishing in July 2021. Her debut historical fiction novel about Ann Lowe, the Black designer of Jackie Kennedy's wedding dress, will release on March 1, 2022, from William Morrow.

She lives in Atlanta, Georgia, with her husband and son.

Kosoko Jackson is a digital media specialist, focusing on digital storytelling, email, social and SMS marketing, and a freelance political journalist. Occasionally, his personal essays and short stories have been featured on Medium, Thought Catalog, and *The Advocate*, and in some literary magazines. His debut rom-com, *I'm So (Not) Over You*, will come out in 2022, published by Berkley, an imprint of Penguin Random House. His Young Adult debut, *Yesterday Is History*, came out in 2021 from SourcebooksFire.

Nicole M. Jackson has a PhD in African American and African Diaspora History. She also writes racially diverse and queer erotica and erotic romance under the pen names Katrina Jackson and Brandy Bush. She likes TV shows that make her cry-laugh, cats, and justice.

Beverly Jenkins is the recipient of the 2017 Romance Writers of America Nora Roberts Lifetime Achievement Award, as well as the 2016 *Romantic Times* Reviewers' Choice Award for historical romance. She has been nominated for the NAACP Image Award in Literature and was featured both in the documentary *Love Between the Covers* and on CBS *Sunday Morning*. Since the publication of *Night Song* in 1994, she's been leading the charge for inclusive romance, and has been a constant darling of reviewers, fans, and her peers alike, garnering accolades for her work from the likes of the *Wall Street Journal, People* magazine, Salon, Shondaland, the *New York Times*, and NPR. She was also named 2018 Author of the Year by the Michigan Library Association. She has forty-nine works in print, and two have been optioned for film by Sony Pictures and Al Roker Entertainment.

Christina C. Jones is a bestselling romance novelist and digital media creator. A timeless storyteller, she is lauded by readers for her ability to seamlessly weave the complexities of modern life into captivating tales of Black romance. As an author, Christina's work has been featured in various media outlets such as *O, The Oprah Magazine, The Griot*, and Shondaland. In addition to her full-time writing career, she cofounded Girl, Have You Read—a popular digital platform that amplifies Black romance authors and their stories. A former graphic designer, Christina has a passion for making things beautiful and can usually be found crafting and cooking in her spare time.

She currently lives in Arkansas with her husband and their two children.

To learn more, visit beingmrsjones.com or follow her across most social media @beingmrsjones.

Julie E. Moody-Freeman is an associate professor in African and Black Diaspora Studies. She received her PhD in Literature and Cultural Studies at the University of Illinois at Chicago. Her teaching and research interests include studies in Black Feminist Theory, the Rhetoric of Colonialism and Post-Colonialism, African American popular romance fiction, and Black Speculative fiction.

Moody-Freeman's publications include co-edited books *The Black Imagination, Science Fiction, and the Speculative* (Routledge, 2011) and *The Black Imagination: Science Fiction, Futurism, and the Speculative* (Peter Lang, 2011) as well as a co-edited special issue of *African and Black Diaspora: An International Journal* (vol. 8, no. 2, July 2015) on "Remapping the Black Atlantic: Diaspora, (Re)Writings of Race and Space." She has also published journal articles and book chapters on Belizean novelist Zee Edgell in *Canadian Woman Studies/les cahiers de la femme* special issue on "Women and the Black Diaspora"; in *MaComère: Journal of the Association of Caribbean Women Writers and Scholars*; in *African Identities*; in *Seeking the Self—Encountering the Other: Diasporic Narrative and the Ethics of Representation*; and in the *Encyclopedia of the African Diaspora*, co-edited by Carole Boyce Davies and Babacar M'bow.

She is the producer and host of the *Black Romance Podcast*, which documents the history of the production and publication of Black Romance through conversations with writers, editors, journalists, and scholars, funded in part by the RWA Academic Research Grant program.

Allie Parker is a writer and podcaster from Washington, DC. A lifelong reader and unapologetic Romance cheerleader, Allie loves talking about Romance books and movies, and does just that on her podcast *Romance Ever After*, which looks at romantic comedies with a genre romance eye.

When she isn't gleefully gabbing about books and movies on her podcast and on Twitter, you can find her futzing around with photography, graphic design, and her plant babies on her front stoop.

Bibliography

Introduction

Bump, Philip. "The Most Likely Person to Read a Book? A College-Educated Black Woman." *The Atlantic*, January 16, 2014. www.theatlantic.com/culture/archive/2014/01/most-likely-person-read-book-college-educated-black-woman/357091/.

Nick and Ari. "The Ripped Bodice's Diversity Report: A Critique." https://nickandari.medium.com/the-ripped-bodices-diversity-report-a-critique-1d0b8f4fbed5.

"The State of Racial Diversity in Romance Publishing Report." www.therippedbodicela.com/state-racial-diversity-romance-publishing-report.

Swartz, Mimi. "Vivian Stephens Helped Turn Romance Writing into a Billion-Dollar Industry. Then She Got Pushed Out." *Texas Monthly*, September 2020. www.texasmonthly.com/arts-entertainment/vivian-stephens-helped-turn-romance-writing-into-billion-dollar-industry/.

A Short History of African American Romance

Hammon, Briton. *A Narrative of the Uncommon Sufferings, and Surprizing Deliverance of Briton Hammon, a Negro Man,—Servant to Gen-*

eral Winslow, of Marshfield, in New-England; Who Returned to Boston, after Having Been Absent Almost Thirteen Years. Containing an Account of the Many Hardships He Underwent from the Time He Left His Master's House, in the Year 1747, to the Time of His Return to Boston.—*How He Was Cast Away in the Capes of Florida;*—*The Horrid Cruelty and Inhuman Barbarity of the Indians in Murdering the Whole Ship's Crew;*—*The Manner of His Being Carry'd by Them into Captivity. Also, an Account of His Being Confined Four Years and Seven Months in a Close Dungeon,*—*and the Remarkable Manner in Which He Met with His Good Old Master in London; Who Returned to New-England, a Passenger in the Same Ship.* Documenting the American South. https://docsouth.unc.edu/neh/hammon/menu.html.

Harper, Frances Ellen Watkins. "We Are All Bound Up Together." Iowa State University Archives of Women's Political Communication. https://awpc.cattcenter.iastate.edu/2017/03/21/we-are-all-bound-up-together-may-1866/.

Prince, Mary. *The History of Mary Prince, a West Indian Slave. Related by Herself. With a Supplement by the Editor. To Which Is Added, the Narrative of Asa-Asa, a Captured African.* Documenting the American South. https://docsouth.unc.edu/neh/prince/menu.html.

Tate, Claudia. *Domestic Allegories of Political Desire: The Black Heroine's Text at the Turn of the Century.* Oxford University Press, 1992.

Imprint

Clark, Kenneth B., and Mamie P. Clark. "Emotional Factors in Racial Identification and Preference in Negro Children." *The Journal of Negro Education* 19, no. 3 (Summer 1950): 341. doi:10.2307/2966491.

I'm Rooting for Everybody Black: Black Solidarity, Black World-Building, and Black Love

Bedi, Sonu. "Sexual Racism: Intimacy as a Matter of Justice." *The Journal of Politics* 77, no. 4 (Oct 2015): 998–1011. http://jstor.org/stable/10.1086/682749.

Bell, Carole V. "The Troubling Gap between Fat Representation and Fat Acceptance in Romance." Book Riot, September 10, 2020. Accessed 2020-09-10. https://bookriot.com/fat-representation-in-romance/.

———. "Women, Film and Racial Thinking: Exploring the Representation and Reception of Interracial Romance." PhD Dissertation, the University of North Carolina at Chapel Hill, 2010.

Clarke, Averil Y. *Inequalities of Love: College-Educated Black Women and the Barriers to Romance and Family.* Politics, History, and Culture. Durham, NC: Duke University Press, 2011.

Cole, Alyssa. "I'm a Romance Novelist Who Writes about Politics—and I Won't 'Stay in My Lane'." *O, The Oprah Magazine*, December 17, 2020. www.oprahdaily.com/entertainment/a34995007/romance-novels-politics-alyssa-cole/.

Collins, Patricia Hill. *Black Feminist Thought: Knowledge, Consciousness, and the Politics of Empowerment.* Routledge Classics. 2nd ed. New York: Routledge, 2009. Table of contents only. www.loc.gov/catdir/toc/ecip0827/2008037553.html.

Dandridge, Rita B. *Black Women's Activism: Reading African American Women's Historical Romances.* African-American Literature and Culture. New York: P. Lang, 2004.

Han, Chong-suk and Kyung-Hee Choi. "Very Few People Say 'No Whites': Gay Men of Color and the Racial Politics of Desire."

Sociological Spectrum 38, no. 3 (2018): 145–61. DOI: 10.1080 /02732173.2018.1469444.

Jackson, Nicole. "Black Love as Activism." *Black Perspectives*, February 28, 2018. www.aaihs.org/black-love-as-activism/.

Rae, Issa. "'I'm Rooting for Everybody Black'—Full Emmys Red Carpet Interview." *Variety*, September 19, 2017. https://youtu.be/WafoKj6MzcU.

Young, Damon. "Hotep, Explained." The Root. www.theroot.com/hotep -explained-1790854506.

Writing in the Gaps: Black Latinx in Romance

Collins, Patricia Hill. *Black Feminist Thought*. New York: Routledge, 2000. p. 27.

Franco, Franklin J. *Los negros, los mulatos y la nación dominicana [Blacks, Mulattos, and the Dominican Nation]*. 11th ed. Santo Domingo, Dominican Republic, 2014. p. 25.

Garifuna. https://en.wikipedia.org/wiki/Garifuna.

Torres-Saillant, Silvio. "The Tribulations of Blackness: Stages in Dominican Racial Identity." *Latin American Perspectives* 100, no. 25.3 (1998): 126–46.

Vicioso, Chiqui. https://es.wikipedia.org/wiki/Chiqui_Vicioso.

How a Black Reader/Author Found Her Romance History

"Beverly Jenkins." *Black Romance Podcast*. Aired September 1, 2020. https://blackromancepodcast.libsyn.com/beverly-jenkins.

"An Extraordinary Union." All About Romance book review. Published April 12, 2017. https://allaboutromance.com/book-review/an -extraordinary-union-by-alyssa-cole/.

Black Cultural Studies and Black Love: Why Black Love Matters

Esensten, Andrew C. "America's Color Line." *The Harvard Crimson*, February 13, 2004. www.thecrimson.com/article/2004/2/13/americas-color-line-on-a-stormy/.

Gates, Henry Louis, Jr. *America Beyond the Color Line*. Episode 4. PBS. Director Daniel Percival. 2004.

hooks, bell. *Salvation: Black People and Love*. New York: Perennial, 2001.

———. *All About Love: New Visions*. New York: Perennial, 2000.

Jacobs, Harriet A. *Incidents in the Life of a Slave Girl: Written by Herself*. Edited by Jean Fagan Yellin. Harvard University Press, 1987.

King, Martin Luther, Jr. *A Testament of Hope: The Essential Writings of Martin Luther King, Jr.* Edited by James Melvin Washington. San Francisco: Harper, 1986.

———. *Strength to Love*. Philadelphia: Fortress Press, 1963.

Lindsey, Treva B. "Cotdamn, Cotdamn: Articulating a Black Women's Politics of Scopic Pleasure in the 21st Century." Presentation in panel The Sweetest Taboo: Theorizing Black Female Pleasure, Agency and Desire within Black Feminism. Conference on Black Portraiture{s} II: Imaging the Black Body and Re-Staging Histories. Florence, Italy. Posted by Mark Anthony Neal, July 2015. www.newblackmaninexile.net/2015/07/the-sweetest-taboo-theorizing-black.html.

Interracial Romance and the Single Story

Livingston, Gretchen, and Anna Brown. "Trends and Patterns in Intermarriage." *Intermarriage in the US 50 Years after* Loving v. Virginia. Pew Research Center. www.pewresearch.org/social-trends /2017/05/18/1-trends-and-patterns-in-intermarriage/.

Tillet, Salamishah. "Interracial Romance, with Black Women as the Stars," *New York Times*, May 22, 2020. https://nytimes.com/2020 /05/22/arts/television/insecure-lovebirds-interracial.html.

Romance Has Broken My Dichotomous Key

Barthes, Roland. *The Pleasure of the Text*. Translated by Richard Miller. New York: Hill and Wang, 1975. (Don't read it, seriously. It's only fifty-some pages, and it's still too long. Barthes is like Vygotsky, in that it's never worth your time to actually read him and a much better use of time to read what other people have to say about him.)

Bishop, Rudine Sims. "Mirrors, Windows, and Sliding Glass Doors." *Perspectives* 6, no. 3 (Summer 1990). (The original is difficult to find, but there is a PDF at https://scenicregional.org/wp-content/uploads /2017/08/Mirrors-Windows-and-Sliding-Glass-Doors.pdf.)

Bump, Philip. "The Most Likely Person to Read a Book? A College-Educated Black Woman." *The Atlantic*, January 16, 2014.

Deahl, Rachel, with Judith Rosen. "New Adult: Needless Marketing-Speak or Valued Subgenre?" *Publishers Weekly*, December 17, 2012.

Gómez, Sarah Hannah (that's me!). "Where Are the People of Color in Dystopias?" Lee & Low Books, *The Open Book Blog*, May 7, 2014.

Naughton, Julie. "New Adult Matures." *Publishers Weekly*, July 14, 2014.

Rosenblatt, Louise M. *Literature as Exploration*. New York: Appleton-Century Company, 1938. The Modern Language Association of America, 5th edition, 1995. (This is actually super interesting, and considering it's nearly 100 years old, it actually reads well and stands up in a lot of ways. Rosenblatt died in 2005 at the age of 101, and honestly, if she had made it a few more years, she probably would have updated it with some more woke race stuff, so I won't even complain about some of the tone-deaf or dated statements in this.)

(Black) Love Is . . . (Black) Love Ain't

Harrison, Da'Shaun. *Belly of the Beast: The Politics of Anti-Fatness as Anti-Blackness*. North Atlantic Books, 2021.

Spillers, Hortense. https://as.vanderbilt.edu/english/bio/hortense-spillers/.

Referenced and Recommended

(IN THE ORDER THEY WERE MENTIONED)

Books

Glory Edim, *Well-Read Black Girl*

Frances Ellen Watkins Harper, *Forest Leaves*

Frances Ellen Watkins Harper, *Iola Leroy, or Shadows Uplifted*

Pauline Hopkins, *Contending Forces*

Kathleen Woodiwiss, *The Flame and the Flower*

Rosalind Welles, *Entwined Destinies*

Sandra Kitt, *Adam and Eva*

Sandra Kitt, *Rites of Spring*

Beverly Jenkins, *Night Song*

Shirley Hailstock, *Clara's Promise*

Patricia Vaughn, *Murmur of Rain*

Helen Fielding, *Bridget Jones's Diary*

Kayla Perrin, *Say You Need Me*

Hanif Abdurraqib, *A Little Devil in America*

Kianna Alexander, Alyssa Cole, Lena Hart, and Piper
Huguley, *Daughters of a Nation: A Black Suffragette
Historical Romance Anthology*

Alyssa Cole, *How to Catch a Queen*

Alyssa Cole, The Loyal League series

Alyssa Cole, The Reluctant Royals series

Alyssa Cole, The Runaway Royals series

Tia Williams, *The Perfect Find*

Charles M. Blow, *The Devil You Know: A Black Power Manifesto*

Alexandria House, The McClain Brothers series

Alexandria House, Romey University series, aka Romey U

Christina C. Jones, *I Think I Might Love You*

Piper Huguley, *Sweet Tea*

K. J. Charles, *A Seditious Affair*

K. J. Charles, *Band Sinister*

Courtney Milan, The Brothers Sinister series

Rebekah Weatherspoon, *Sated*

Rebekah Weatherspoon, *So Sweet*

Rebekah Weatherspoon, *At Her Feet*

Alyssa Cole, *That Could Be Enough*

Alyssa Cole, *Once Ghosted, Twice Shy*

Alyssa Cole, *How to Find a Princess*

Talia Hibbert, *Take a Hint, Dani Brown*

Chencia C. Higgins, *Things Hoped For*

Chencia C. Higgins, *Consolation Gifts*

Meka James, *Being Hospitable*

J. Nichole, *A Girl Like Me*

Christina C. Jones, *Something Like Love*

G. L. Tomas, *Wander This World*

G. L. Tomas, *The Love Bet*

Ann Allen Shockley, *Loving Her*

Ann Allen Shockley, *Say Jesus and Come to Me*

Ann Allen Shockley, *The Black and White of It*

Frank Yerby, *The Saracen Blade*

Margaret Irwin, *Elizabeth, Captive Princess*

Margaret Campbell Barnes, *The Passionate Brood*

W. E. B. Du Bois, *Dark Princess: A Romance*

Octavia E. Butler, *Wild Seed*

Torquato Tasso, *Gerusalemme liberata*

Ludovico Ariosto, *Orlando Furioso*

Edmund Spenser, *The Faerie Queene*

Heliodorus of Emesa, *Aethiopica*

Bertrice Small, *The Kadin*

Naima Simone, *Back in the Texan's Bed*

Vanessa Riley, *The Butterfly Bride*

Vanessa Riley, *The Bittersweet Bride*

Vanessa Riley, *A Duke, the Lady, and a Baby*

Vanessa Riley, *An Earl, the Girl, and a Toddler*

Katrina Jackson, *Office Hours*

Francis Ray, *Only You*

Rebekah Weatherspoon, *Harbor*

Vanessa Riley, *The Bewildered Bride*

Alyssa Cole, *Agnes Moor's Wild Knight*

Beverly Jenkins, *Indigo*

Elysabeth Grace, *Fate's Consort*

Elysabeth Grace, *Your Heart Only*

Referenced and Recommended

Gloria Naylor, *Mama Day*

bell hooks, *All About Love: New Visions*

Frances Smith Foster, editor, *Love and Marriage in Early African America*

Michael Eric Dyson, *Why I Love Black Women*

Audre Lorde, *Sister Outsider*

Treva B. Lindsey, *Colored No More: Reinventing Black Womanhood in Washington, D.C.*

James Weldon Johnson, *The Autobiography of an Ex-Colored Man*

Piper Huguley, *A Virtuous Ruby*

Piper Huguley, *A Most Precious Pearl*

Piper Huguley, *A Treasure of Gold*

Piper Huguley, *A Champion's Heart*

Piper Huguley, Home to Milford College series

Piper Huguley, *A Sweet Way to Freedom*

Alice Walker, *The Color Purple*

Sister Souljah, *The Coldest Winter Ever*

Beverly Jenkins, *Destiny's Surrender*

Farrah Rochon, New York Sabers series

Alyssa Cole, *Let It Shine*

Sandra Kitt, *The Color of Love*

Jasmine Guillory, The Wedding Date series

Alexa Martin, *Intercepted*

Alexis Daria, *You Had Me at Hola*

Farrah Rochon, *The Boyfriend Project*

Film and Television

The Bodyguard

West Side Story

A Warm December

Carmen Jones

Jem and the Holograms

To All the Boys I've Loved
   Before

Sylvie's Love

Lovers Rock

Being Mary Jane

The Color Purple

The Watermelon Woman

Pariah

Living Single

Quinceañera

Xica da Silva

Black in Latin America

America beyond the Color
   Line

Love Jones

Degrassi: The Next
   Generation

Chilling Adventures of
   Sabrina

The Bold Type

Pose

The Incredible Jessica James

Bridgerton

Guess Who

Romeo Must Die

The Lovebirds

Juanita

Something New

The Jeffersons

A Different World

The Fresh Prince of Bel-Air

Hangin' with Mr. Cooper

The Wayans Bros.

The Jamie Foxx Show

Sister, Sister

Moesha

The Parkers

One on One

Girlfriends

Half & Half

The Game

Atlanta

Queen Sugar

Insecure

Online

Well-Read Black Girl Book Club. www.wellreadblackgirl.com.

Coffee Bookshelves. https://coffeebookshelves.com.

Women of Color in Romance. www.wocinromance.com.

Sistah Girls Book Club. http://shareehereford.com/latest
-updates/book-club-for-sistah-girls/.

Black Romance Podcast. https://blackromancepodcast
.libsyn.com.

Girl, Have You Read. http://girlhaveyouread.com.

Photo by James Galloway-Reed

Jessica P. Pryde is a contributing editor for Book Riot, where she is the cohost of the *When in Romance* podcast and writes about bookish things of all kinds. Having earned an AB in the Interdisciplinary Project in the Humanities at Washington University in St. Louis and her MLIS at San José State University, she is now a librarian for a public library system in Southern Arizona, where she lives with her husband and an ever-growing collection of Funko Pop!s. More information on her writing, including links to her online work, can be found on her website. *Black Love Matters* is her first book.

CONNECT ONLINE

JessicaPryde.com

🐦 JessIsReading

📷 Jess_Is_Reading